I0104723

Enhancing the Oversight Impact of Chile's Supreme Audit Institution

APPLYING BEHAVIOURAL INSIGHTS FOR PUBLIC INTEGRITY

))) OECD

BETTER POLICIES FOR BETTER LIVES

This document, as well as any data and map included herein, are without prejudice to the status of or sovereignty over any territory, to the delimitation of international frontiers and boundaries and to the name of any territory, city or area.

Please cite this publication as:
OECD (2022), *Enhancing the Oversight Impact of Chile's Supreme Audit Institution: Applying Behavioural Insights for Public Integrity*, OECD Public Governance Reviews, OECD Publishing, Paris, https://doi.org/10.1787/1afdc85e-en.

ISBN 978-92-64-86294-4 (print)
ISBN 978-92-64-83598-6 (pdf)
ISBN 978-92-64-42227-8 (HTML)
ISBN 978-92-64-64284-3 (epub)

OECD Public Governance Reviews
ISSN 2219-0406 (print)
ISSN 2219-0414 (online)

Foreword

Insights from behavioural sciences are increasingly applied to improve our understanding of how cognitive biases and social dynamics shape the decisions and behaviour of people to increase the impact of public policies. The majority of these applications have been concerned with improving policy implementation and changing individual behaviour.

While considering psychological factors in auditing and in related fields of accounting and law enforcement is not new, there is still significant scope for Supreme Audit Institutions (SAI) to systematically apply behavioural insights to improve the impact of their work. In the context of social, economic and environmental crises, where governments must ensure that public resources are spent both efficiently and effectively, SAIs play a key role by providing not only oversight but also insight and strategic vision. SAIs can thus support public administrations in achieving the desired impact of policies for citizens.

Over the past two decades, Chile's SAI, the Office of the General Comptroller of the Republic of Chile (CGR), has undertaken several initiatives to broaden its traditional oversight role towards a more collaborative one that helps public organisations improve their processes and services. Since 2017, the CGR has promoted a Compliance Support Programme; nonetheless, it still faces challenges in ensuring that public organisations take corrective actions in response to the audit findings. This transformation is also reflected in CGR's Strategic Plan 2021-2024. Striving to find innovative solutions to improve its own work, the CGR worked with the OECD to use behavioural insights to improve the uptake of its audit reports and engaged in a thorough review of its audit and audit follow-up processes, applying OECD's BASIC methodology (Behaviour, Analysis, Strategies, Intervention, and Change).

This report is part of OECD's work to help countries effectively implement the *OECD Recommendation on Public Integrity*. It applies, for the first time, a systematic behavioural lens to external auditing. Building on previous OECD work with the CGR, the report focuses on the auditors and the auditees in Chile -- their perceptions, attitudes and behaviour -- to provide concrete recommendations on how the CGR can promote a better uptake of their reports, in particular by moving from audits focusing on detecting irregularities to audits that seek to provide guidance to the public administration. The goal is to improve institutional performance and, ultimately, the lives of Chilean citizens.

The report was reviewed by the OECD Working Party of Senior Public Integrity Officials (SPIO) on 13 April 2022. It was approved by the Public Governance Committee on 5 May 2022 and prepared for publication by the Secretariat.

Acknowledgements

The report was prepared by the Directorate of Public Governance under the leadership of Elsa Pilichowski, OECD Director for Public Governance (GOV), and Julio Bacio Terracino, Head of GOV's Public Sector Integrity Division. The report was co-ordinated and drafted by Frédéric Boehm. Gavin Ugale, Giulio Nessi, Maria Camila Porras and Cristián Picón provided invaluable support and inputs. Editorial and administrative assistance was provided by Meral Gedik.

The OECD thanks the Comptroller General of the Republic of Chile, Jorge Andrés Bermúdez Soto, the Head of the Audit Division, Eduardo Díaz, as well as the team of the Office of the Comptroller General that has supported this project, María De Los Ángeles Donoso Rivas, Carlos Eduardo Márquez Gutiérrez, Osvaldo Cristian Rudloff Pulgar, Nicolás Alberto Vega Cohen, Ernesto García San Martín, Eduardo Díaz Araya, Nicolás Francisco Lagos Machuca, Valeria Edith Torres Godoy and Daniela Francisca Santana Silva for the many fruitful discussions, their inputs and feedback on preliminary findings and recommendations as well as for their support in organising the virtual fact-finding throughout the project. The OECD would also like to thank the individuals and organisations at national, regional and municipal level, who were interviewed and took part in the process by providing information for the elaboration of the report, in particular the Ministry of Defense's Subsecretariat of the Armed Forces (*Subsecretaria para las Fuerzas Armadas*), the Ministry of Housing and Urbanism (*Ministerio de Vivienda y Urbanismo*), the National Kindergarten Board (*Junta Nacionales de Jardines Infantiles*), the Chilean Antarctic Institute (*Instituto Antártico Chileno*), the Regional Government of Arica y Parinacota, the Municipalities of Rio Claro, Quilicura and Vichuquen, as well as the Universities of Chile and Santiago de Chile.

The OECD further thanks the peer reviewers who read and commented on different versions of this report. Their comments and perspectives have significantly contributed to strengthening the report: Ina den Haan, Netherlands Court of Audit (*Algemene Rekenkamer*), Carolina Souto Carballido, Comptroller General of the Union of Brazil (*Controladoria Geral da Uniao*, CGU), Bernagie Steven, Belgian Court of Audit (*Rekenhof*), Franisco Silva, Civil Service of Chile (*Servicio Civil Chile*) and Sebastián Gil. Preliminary findings and recommendations were discussed with Miguel Peñailillo and at the internal OECD Behavioural Science Meetup, with special thanks to Chiara Varazzini, James Drummond, Trish Lavery and Guillermo Morales for their feedback.

Table of contents

FIGURES

TABLES

Follow OECD Publications on:

http://twitter.com/OECD_Pubs

http://www.facebook.com/OECDPublications

http://www.linkedin.com/groups/OECD-Publications-4645871

http://www.youtube.com/oecdilibrary

http://www.oecd.org/oecddirect/

Executive summary

Supreme Audit Institutions (SAI) are a key part of the institutional framework of democratic and accountable states. Audit reports are one of the main vehicles through which SAIs can induce change in the public sector. To do so, audit reports and their observations and recommendations must be relevant, read and understood by the right people, made available at the right time, and the presented in the right way.

Understanding the behaviour of both auditors and auditees is thus a crucial part of analysing the follow-up of audit reports -- or the lack thereof. Applying behavioural insights can identify avenues for improving the uptake of audit reports and help enhance the impact of SAIs. The report identifies relevant behaviours, perceptions and attitudes of the involved stakeholders to understand the behavioural drivers underlying non-compliance with their audit reports and provides concrete recommendations to address these issues.

Main findings

The report first reviews previous research on behavioural barriers and biases of both auditors and auditees that can help explain the success or the failure of audits to achieve the desired impact. Auditing is principally a matter of human judgement and, as such, is not immune to typical biases. In turn, auditees, too, may react differently to audit results depending on the way these are collected, processed, presented and communicated.

The CGR has made significant progress over the past years in monitoring the follow-up of audit reports. In 2012, the CGR established audit follow-up units, followed in 2014 by the online follow-up system SICA (*Sistema Integrado para el Control de Auditorias*) and, in 2016, the Compliance Support Programme. Thanks to these initiatives, the CGR found out that, on average, around 49% of the audit observations are addressed by the audited entities. Applying the behavioural lens to understand the implementation rate, the project confirmed several insights suggested by research and that help explain the implementation rate in Chile:

- The quantity of audit observations and the way they are presented to auditees undermine their perceived relevance, can trigger "decision fatigue" and sometimes produce a negative attitude towards audits in general. In particular, the quantity of detailed observations makes it difficult to for auditees to see the bigger picture and understand the underlying issues driving these observations.
- Perceptions of unfairness by auditees and weaknesses in communication between auditors and auditees during the audit process can lead to observations that could have been avoided and may undermine the willingness of auditees to address audit findings. Some of the challenges in communication are driven by an informal culture within the CGR that still primes primes auditors to take a "severe" approach to auditees and informally pressures them to include a large number of findings in the reports.
- Heads of services and public managers in the audited services sometimes show low levels of interest in, ownership of, and motivation to address audit results. This can be partly explained by the fact that non-compliance with audit observations seldom has negative consequences.

However, the technical or legal nature of the observations helps explain a lack of interest by leaders, both at senior and middle management levels, as the strategic value of the audits remain unclear.

Main recommendations

Based on these findings, the report suggests undertaking a behaviourally inspired review of existing procedures and practices to enhance the uptake of audit recommendations. The measures are complementary and aim for impact at three levels.

- First, the CGR could seek to improve the auditor-auditee relationship by increasing interactions between them and making these interactions more constructive. In addition, the CGR could continue promoting an internal cultural change towards more supportive attitudes towards auditees.

- Second, focusing on the drafting and communication of the audit reports could help improve their uptake. In particular, this requires a review of the way audit reports are drafted and could be complemented by testing different messages to communicate about the audit report.

- Third, the CGR could target the follow-up process and allow for better planning by auditees, by introducing some flexibility in deadlines and by tracking progreess. Such steps should help reduce frustration and promote better quality responses.

The report proposes a detailed theory of change and implementation design to test a combination of two specific measures in a pilot to be carried out in audits at municipal level. The first is a pre-follow up meeting during which the CGR explains and clarifies the audit reports. This should reduce the cognitive burden caused by audit reports that are too complex. The second would allow some flexibility in the deadlines to address the audit observations. This should reduce the stress and perceived unfairness reported by auditees.

1 What drives the impact of Supreme Audit Institutions

Audit reports issued by Supreme Audit Institutions are key in generating impact, as they are the main vehicle through which audits can induce change in the public sector. As such, implementation rates of audit recommendations from audit reports are instrumental to achieve impact. This chapter provides a brief overview on the various factors that help explaining the implementation rate of audit recommendations before focusing in detail on relevant behavioural drivers of both auditors and auditees.

Introduction

In line with international standards as well as good practices promoted by the International Organisation of Supreme Audit Institutions (INTOSAI) and the OECD, Supreme Audit Institutions (SAI) should lead by example and demonstrate their added value and impact (INTOSAI, 2019[1]). In particular, the audit reports are key in generating impact, as they are the main vehicle through which audits can induce change in the public sector. To do so, audit reports and their observations and recommendations have to be relevant, have to be read and understood by the right people, they have to be available at the right time and the information has to be presented in the right way. As such, INTOSAI invites SAIs to continually review how they can make their reports more readable, more accessible, and more relevant to all stakeholders (INTOSAI, 2010[2]). In turn, INTOSAI's Development Initiative (IDI) works with the SAI to support them in applying the standards, to build capacities and to ensure the quality of audits, for instance in the context of the Facilitating Audit Impact (FAI) strategy (IDI, 2021[3]).

Chile's SAI, the Comptroller General of the Republic (*Contraloría General de la República*, CGR) faces the same pressure as other SAIs to generate and show impact. The Constitution establishes the CGR as an autonomous government body, which has a high level of organisational and administrative independence. The CGR has made significant progress over the last decade and has, amongst others, reviewed the monitoring and follow-up processes of its audit reports; also with support from the OECD (OECD, 2014[4]; OECD, 2016[5]). Thanks to the audit follow-up units (*Unidades de Seguimiento*), created by the CGR in 2012, the Integrated System for Audit Control (*Sistema Integrado para el Control de Auditorías*, SICA) and the Compliance Support Programme (Chapter 2), the CGR found out, however, that between 2015 and 2020, on average, only 50% of the audit observations included in their compliance audit reports were addressed by the audited entities.

Consequently, the CGR took several measures aimed at improving the uptake of audit reports. For instance, the Compliance Support Programme (*Programa de Apoyo al Cumplimiento*, PAC) was launched in 2016 with the objective to identify and implement creative mechanisms to increase the rate of observations addressed by audited entities. In 2019, the CGR conducted an internal evaluation exercise, which showed that public entities were satisfied with this initiative and find it useful. Learning from these insights, the CGR is exploring new mechanisms to enhance the impact of this initiative in the context of the 2021-2024 Strategic Planning.

In this context and striving to better understand and find innovative solutions to improve the level of uptake of the audit reports, the CGR collaborated with the OECD to apply a behavioural perspective. A behavioural perspective is an inductive approach that combines behavioural insights (BI) from psychology, cognitive science and social science with empirically tested results to discover how humans actually make choices. The perspective is increasingly used to improve our understanding of how context, cognitive biases and other influences affect the behaviour of people, including behaviours related to integrity policies (OECD, 2019[6]; OECD, 2018[7]).

Following up on audit reports, or failing to do so (at all or in a timely manner), is also the product of human behaviour. In a nutshell, within a given institutional and regulatory context, a public official receives the audit report, reads it, has to understand and process the information provided there and ultimately has to decide to act based on this information; if at all, to what extent, how and given the constraints the official is facing. To understand who these individuals are and why they behave as they do is thus relevant for informing improvements that could positively influence the uptake of CGR's audit reports. Considering psychological factors in auditing and in related fields of accounting and law enforcement is not new (Kida, 1984[8]; Kinney and Uecker, 1982[9]; Kassin, Dror and Kukucka, 2013[10]). However, a recent OECD review of BI applications around the world did not find examples of interventions focusing on auditing processes, but some examples of applications aimed at ensuring compliance with rules or regulations could be relevant to inspire interventions in the audit world (OECD, 2017[11]).

To analyse the Chilean context and develop proposals for behavioural interventions, the project follows the BASIC methodology, developed by the OECD to support policymakers with tools, methods and ethical guidelines for conducting BI projects (OECD, 2019[6]). BASIC follows and inductive, context-driven approach (Figure 1.1).

Figure 1.1. The BASIC framework in the context of the CGR-OECD project

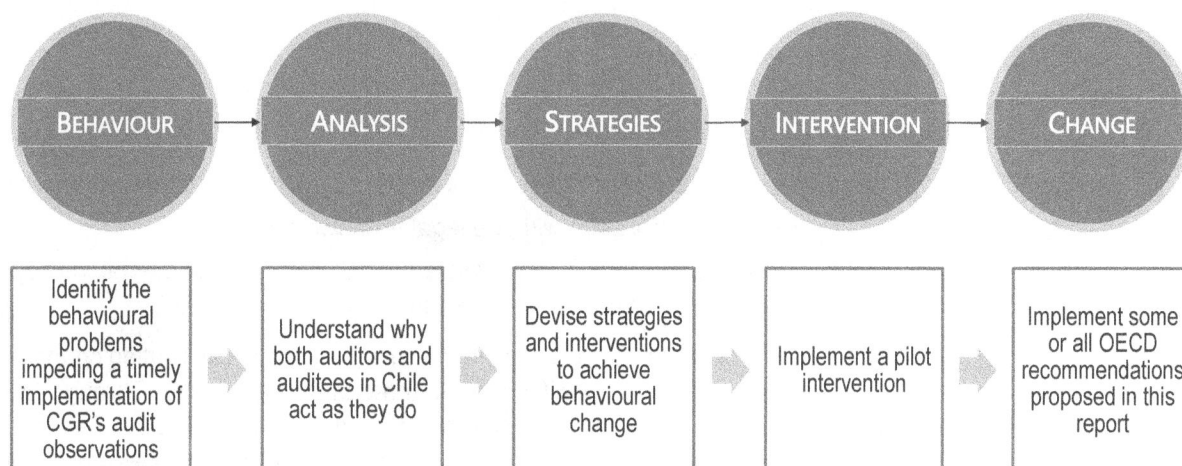

BEHAVIOUR	ANALYSIS	STRATEGIES	INTERVENTION	CHANGE
Identify the behavioural problems impeding a timely implementation of CGR's audit observations	Understand why both auditors and auditees in Chile act as they do	Devise strategies and interventions to achieve behavioural change	Implement a pilot intervention	Implement some or all OECD recommendations proposed in this report

Source: (OECD, 2019[6])

To identify the actors' relevant behaviours and to understand the context in Chile that is shaping these behaviours (steps B and A of the BASIC framework), the project carried out an in-depth qualitative analysis based on a desk research and various fact-finding interviews and focus group discussions with key stakeholders. A quantitative analysis of the observations included in the audit reports complemented the qualitative research (Chapter 2). Due to COVID-19, the OECD carried out the qualitative research through video conferences. Interviews focused on public officials responsible for internal audit and on public managers within public entities at national and at municipal level. The CGR formed a team of experts dedicated to the project, providing information and feedback and participating in meetings organised and moderated by the OECD. Based on this analysis, Chapter 3 provides a set of concrete interventions to address them (step S of the BASIC framework).

Before moving to the specific context in Chile, this chapter provides a brief discussion of the role audit reports play for the impact of SAI, as well as the various factors driving the uptake of audit reports by audited entities and thus their potential to generate change in the public administration. Finally, the chapter focuses on behavioural aspects from both auditors and auditees that are relevant for explaining the uptake of audit reports.

Defining and measuring the impact of SAI

The role of SAIs in the promotion of good governance has evolved over the last decades, moving from activities that are essentially compliance-oriented to a role aimed at understanding and enhancing the performance of governments to deliver for citizens. This change has led to a diversification of SAI's strategic objectives, audits and advisory role to include the provision of evidence-based insights and foresight in support of decision-making, as a complement to traditional oversight activities (OECD,

2016[12]). Government-wide performance audits and data-driven dashboards that track or predict economic changes are just some examples of insight and foresight activities.

This evolving role brings new challenges for SAIs to measure their impact. For SAIs that traditionally focus on financial and compliance audits, as in Chile, measuring impact largely focuses on output-based indicators, such as the number of audits undertaken or clean audit opinions without irregularities. Going beyond the output level, the impact of a SAI in terms of relevant outcomes could be measured, for example, in terms of:

- savings due to the measures implemented;
- increases in revenue;
- reductions in expenditure;
- increases in satisfaction with the delivery of public services delivered by the public administration;
- providing legal certainty by ensuring compliance with the legal frameworks; or
- improvements in achieving other policy goals, e.g. related to SDGs (environmental quality, education, health, gender equality, anti-corruption and integrity etc.)

One of the main challenges for SAIs to measure their impact is the difficulty they face in attributing changes in outcome levels in audited entities and society to specific actions and outputs of the SAI. Through the audit reports, a SAI is able to influence the audited entities and promote change that, ultimately, can lead to the desired impact at outcome levels (Figure 1.2). The outputs of the SAI in terms, for example, of number of audits, audit reports published or the number of recommendations issued, can be measured and clearly attributed to the SAI and are under its direct control. Yet, how the auditees use these outputs of SAIs is beyond their direct control, but is critical to reach the higher-level desired outcome at the level of the auditees in the public administration and in the effective and efficient provision of public services.

Figure 1.2. Simplified generic theory of change of Supreme Audit Institutions

For example, an audit report (SAI output) may contribute to improve user satisfaction of a public service (outcome). But a potential impact at this outcome level stemming from an audit report must have passed by actions taken by the auditee: for instance, that a public entity providing services to citizens implements the audit recommendations (intermediate outcome). Of course, user satisfaction depends on a wide variety of factors and not only the uptake of the audit report by the auditee. To what degree, if at all, is it possible to attribute an observed increase in customer satisfaction to the changes implemented thanks to the audit reports? Would the changes in user satisfaction perhaps even have occurred without these audit reports? Without a counterfactual, these questions are difficult to answer.

In turn, assuming that the audits are carried out following professional standards and that audit reports include relevant observations and recommendations, the impact of SAIs at the level of the intermediate outcome, that is, the uptake of the audit reports by the auditee, is more straightforward to establish. At this level, the impact can be measured by the rate of implementation, understood as the percentage of corrected observations or implemented recommendations included in the audit reports.

Following this logic, the rate of implementation is a good proxy indicator for the potential success of external audit and for measuring the immediate uptake of audit reports. Due to its significant instrumental value, this report focuses on ways to influence this indicator.

Nonetheless, the indicator has some drawbacks. For instance, it is relevant to distinguish between types of audit. Financial and compliance audits usually result in administrative, procedural observations that are relatively easy to pinpoint and to follow-up through the rate of implementation. Performance audits, in turn, typically result in recommendations concerning policy design or implementation that are more difficult to track. Other points to keep in mind are:

- The rate of implementation, as discussed, only reveals tangible instrumental impact, neglecting the other types of impact at the outcome level, both at the public entity and societal level.
- The indicator does not take into account the relative importance (in financial or societal terms) of the observations or recommendations and the complexity of implementing them.
- Often, some improvements are already implemented during the (and as a result of) an ongoing audit. In this case, auditors will not formulate any recommendations, although there has been impact.
- Quality of recommendations matter. Implementing recommendations does not necessarily lead to improvements and not implementing recommendations is not always a bad, if their quality is not adequate (Desmedt et al., 2017[13]).

Factors that influence the uptake of audit reports by auditees

A variety of factors is likely to determine whether an audited entity in the public sector is willing and able to address observations or implement changes recommended through external audit by a SAI. Research and international good practice, reflected in international standards promoted by national and international organisations, emphasise three groups of variables that are key in explaining impact of SAIs (Figure 1.3). A first group includes factors related to the audit process itself ("Micro-level"), a second group considers factors that are related to the SAI and the audited entities ("Meso-level") and a third group considers different pressure groups outside the audited entity ("Macro-level").

Figure 1.3. Factors influencing the impact of performance audits conducted by SAIs

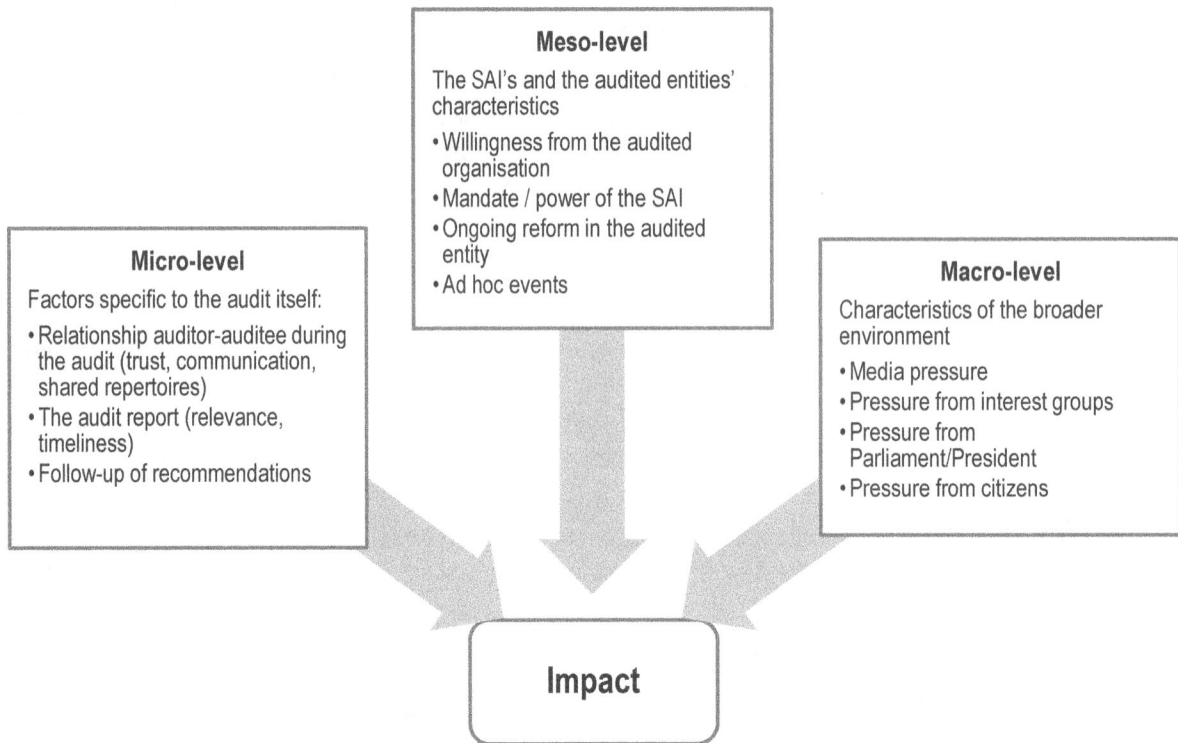

Meso-level

The SAI's and the audited entities' characteristics
- Willingness from the audited organisation
- Mandate / power of the SAI
- Ongoing reform in the audited entity
- Ad hoc events

Micro-level

Factors specific to the audit itself:
- Relationship auditor-auditee during the audit (trust, communication, shared repertoires)
- The audit report (relevance, timeliness)
- Follow-up of recommendations

Macro-level

Characteristics of the broader environment
- Media pressure
- Pressure from interest groups
- Pressure from Parliament/President
- Pressure from citizens

Impact

Source: (Van Loocke and Put, 2011[14]).

Understanding these drivers helps to identify entry points for concrete measures aimed at increasing the uptake of audit reports and therefore, indirectly, the impact of the SAI in promoting change. On the one hand, SAIs can optimise factors that are under their direct control, such as the auditor-auditee relationship during the audit process itself, the audit report and the follow-up processes. For instance, at the micro-level, a study in Belgium found that, in particular, a fluent communication, openness between auditors and entities and the level of recognition of the credibility and legitimacy of the auditees are relevant in explaining impact (Desmedt and Pattyn, 2015[15]). As stressed by EUROSAI, "audit findings should be discussed with the auditee before commencing with the formulation of conclusions and recommendations" (EUROSAI, 2021[16]). In the survey conducted by EUROSAI on the uptake of audit recommendations, 27 out of 33 respondents from European SAIs are basing their recommendation on a dialogue with auditees.

On the other hand, for factors that are outside their direct range of influence, SAIs can develop strategies aimed at indirectly influencing auditees. At the meso-level, the same study found that the position of the auditors' recommendations within the management priorities, the will of the authorities and the political will were also found to be significant in the Belgian context (Desmedt and Pattyn, 2015[15]). At the macro-level, for example, a SAI can try to establish alliances with other actors or favour processes that improve its image in the media, in the legislative or in the executive to promote outside pressure to ensure that auditees are following up on audit reports. Stakeholders should be engaged as early as the planning phase of an audit process.

Publicly tracking actions taken by the executive to take action based on audit reports may also contribute to create pressure at the macro level. Studies in Brazil found that making audit results from the Office of Comptroller-General (*Controladoria Geral da União*, CGU) public, significantly reduced the probability of re-electing a mayor in which at least two violations associated with corruption were reported (Ferraz and Finan, 2008[17]; Avis, Ferraz and Finan, 2018[18]).[1] In OECD countries with available data, 65.2% of the countries make this information public, while only 25% of countries in Latin America with available data do so – amongst them Brazil (Figure 1.4).

Figure 1.4. While 65.2% of OECD countries publicly report on actions taken by the executive to address audit recommendations, only 25% of countries in Latin America do so

Does either the Supreme Audit Institution (SAI) or legislature release to the public a report that tracks actions taken by the executive to address audit recommendations?

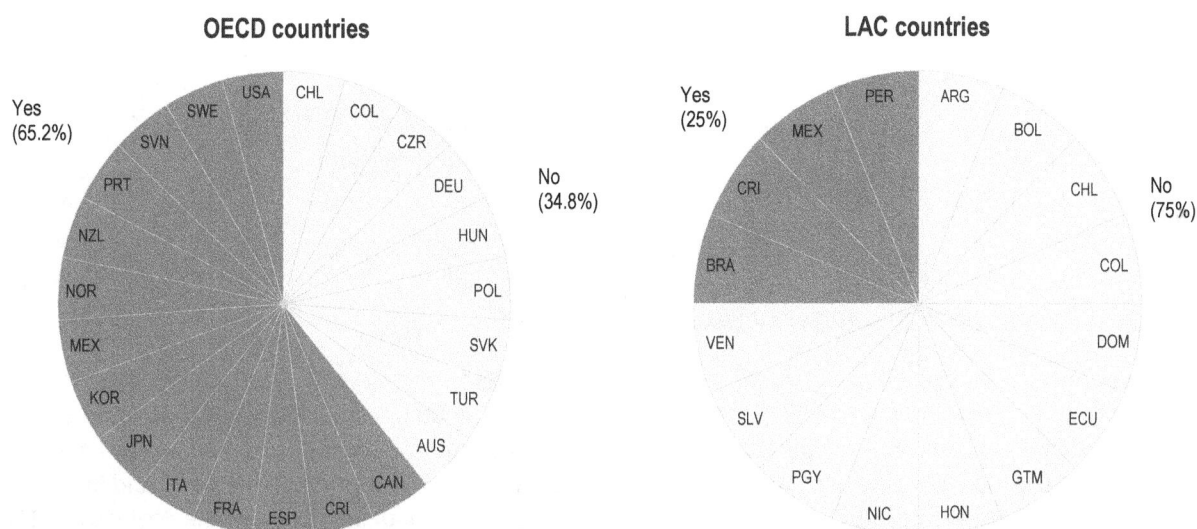

Note: The graphs above counted as "Yes" all countries responding that "Yes, the SAI or legislature reports publicly on what steps the executive has taken to address all/most/some audit recommendations" (score 100 for "all", 67 for "most" or 33 for "some").
Source: International Budget Partnership, Open Budget Survey 2019

Nonetheless, behind the percentage of corrected observations or implemented recommendations included in the audit reports there are, in the end, human beings in the audited entities that take a decision on whether to take action, or to what degree. These individuals are operating in a given normative and cultural context, which provides incentives and shapes their decisions. There may be legal obligations to implement audit observations or recommendations as well as sanctions in case of non-compliance. In addition, the relevance and quality of the provided audit reports will influence whether they are likely to trigger implementation or not. As mentioned in the introduction, psychological aspects, explored in the following section, may also influence these behaviours of auditees.

How behavioural insights contribute to explaining the uptake of audit reports

Behavioural barriers and biases of both the auditor and the auditee can help explaining the success or the failure of audits to achieve the desired impact. Figure 1.5 provides an overview of behavioural insights, explored in more detail in the following section. By integrating these behavioural insights into auditing processes, SAIs could better anticipate the behavioural implications of their audits and use these insights to design and deliver more effective audit processes and reports that are more likely to be followed-up, lead to change and therefore to improve the welfare of citizens.

Figure 1.5. Main behavioural insights related to auditing

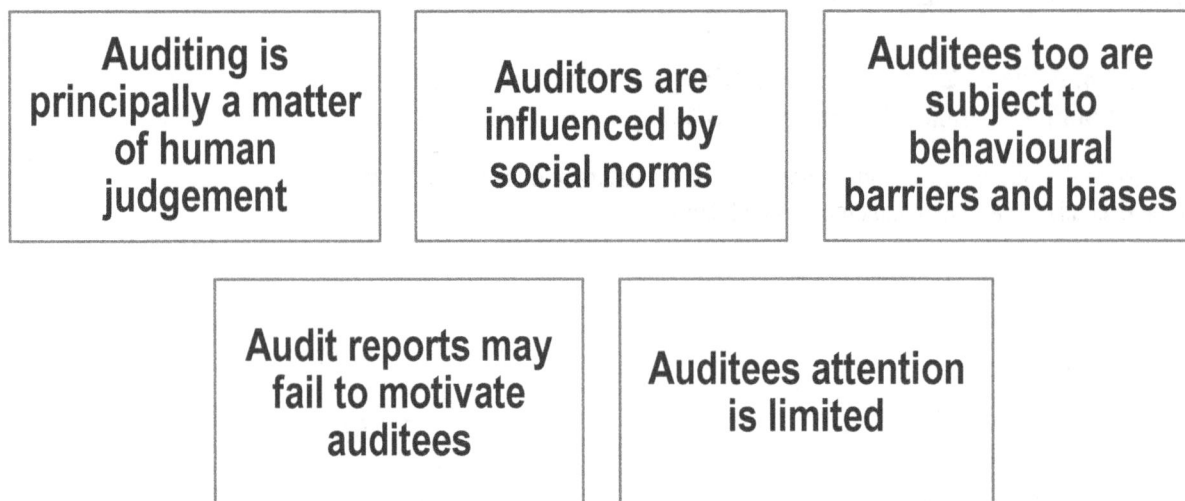

Auditing is principally a matter of human judgement	**Auditors are influenced by social norms**	**Auditees too are subject to behavioural barriers and biases**
Audit reports may fail to motivate auditees	**Auditees attention is limited**	

Auditing is principally a matter of human judgement

Independence and objectivity are fundamental values of SAIs. They are defined in the International Standards of Supreme Audit Institutions as being "free from circumstances or influences that compromise, or may be seen as compromising, professional judgement, and to act in an impartial and unbiased manner" (INTOSAI, 2019[19]). Nonetheless, auditing is principally a matter of human judgement and as such, objectivity is not always possible. In fact, the subjective judgment of auditors is part of the profession. The International Standards on Auditing (ISA), through ISA 200, define professional judgement as the "application of relevant training, knowledge and experience (...) in making informed decisions about the courses of action that are appropriate in the circumstances of the audit engagement." The fundamental Principles of Public-Sector Auditing (ISSAI 100) emphasises that professional judgement implies the application of collective knowledge, skills and experience to the audit process (INTOSAI, 2019[20]). Professional judgment, as defined in ISA 200 or ISSAI 100, is also relevant when it comes to assessing the audit findings and the prioritisation of audit observations and recommendations. As such, subjective judgement, just as professional criticism, plays a fundamental part in informing the auditor's analysis.

However, insights from behavioural sciences show that judgements may also be subject to systematic cognitive biases that could become relevant when carrying out an audit. For example, audit criteria help to guide auditors in their analysis and judgements. Nonetheless, as human beings, our desires powerfully influence the way we interpret information, even when we are trying to be objective and impartial (Bazerman, Moore and Loewenstein, 2002[21]).

Audit criteria can only resolve this partially. Despite the fact that audit criteria may provide guidance for relative objectivity, auditing leaves considerable leeway for ambiguity. For instance, confirmation bias may be an issue when auditors have pre-conceived ideas about the audited institution or the processes. Their audit may then unconsciously focus on details that confirm their existing beliefs. In fact, confirmation bias could affect objective judgment in both directions: against or in favour of the auditee. Research showed, indeed, that the degree in which auditors tend to support the auditee ("advocacy attitude") influences the quality of the evidence collected by biasing auditors' initial judgments and influencing the type of subsequent evidence collected. Such a confirmation bias exists in particular for low advocacy auditors, i.e. auditors with low levels of support for auditees, as they tend to plan a less objective search for more confirmatory evidence, potentially demonstrating too much presumption of distrust in management ("presumptive doubt") (Pennington, Schafer and Pinsker, 2017[22]).

Auditors should strive to have neutral initial beliefs. Unconsciously, however, cognitive biases could affect our pre-existing beliefs and undermine our way to draw conclusions because of anecdotes we hear, our insensitivity to sample size or our tendency to overestimate our ability to interpret and predict outcomes given a set of information (the illusion of validity). Overconfidence of the auditors may further undermine the accuracy of the auditor's judgements.

For example, perceptions and stories about corrupt and inefficient public administrations could frame auditors towards gathering evidence and over-emphasising information that is unfavourable to auditees, resulting in recommendations that are no longer objective. Such a confirmation bias against auditees perhaps may not be problematic in areas of high corruption and fraud risks, but could become problematic for low-risk audits (Pennington, Schafer and Pinsker, 2017[22]). It certainly will make it more difficult to motivate auditees and to build a constructive climate between auditors and auditees. The auditees could perceive the cognitive biases that are undermining auditors' professional judgement. This, in turn, could delegitimise the audit recommendations and, consequently, create resistance to follow-up on audit reports.

Auditors are influenced by social norms

Expectations about the "right" behaviour can also influence auditors. Auditors are part of a social group, which can be the auditor's unit, the SAI they are working in or even the auditor profession as a whole. What auditors believe most other auditors in their group are actually doing (empirical expectation) or what they believe most other auditors of their group expect them to do (normative expectation) can explain behavioural pattern and are called "social norms" (Bicchieri, 2005[23]; Bicchieri, 2017[24]). Such social norms can be extremely powerful in shaping behaviours.

Figure 1.6 describes how to diagnose an observed pattern of behaviour (Bicchieri, 2017[24]). On the one hand, there are of course reasons why people follow behavioural patterns no matter what others do, either because it serves a purpose (custom) or because it is thought to be the right thing to do (moral norm). On the other hand, the social group becomes relevant if the behaviour of an individual depends on what others do (descriptive norm) or what is believed to be expected, and potentially punished in case the rule is not respected (social norm). If such social norms are relevant in explaining behaviour, interventions that only aim at changing the formal rules or that aim at appealing to what is the "correct thing" to do, may fail in changing behaviours (Bicchieri, Lindemans and Jiang, 2014[25]; Yamin et al., 2019[26]).

Figure 1.6. Diagnosing social norms

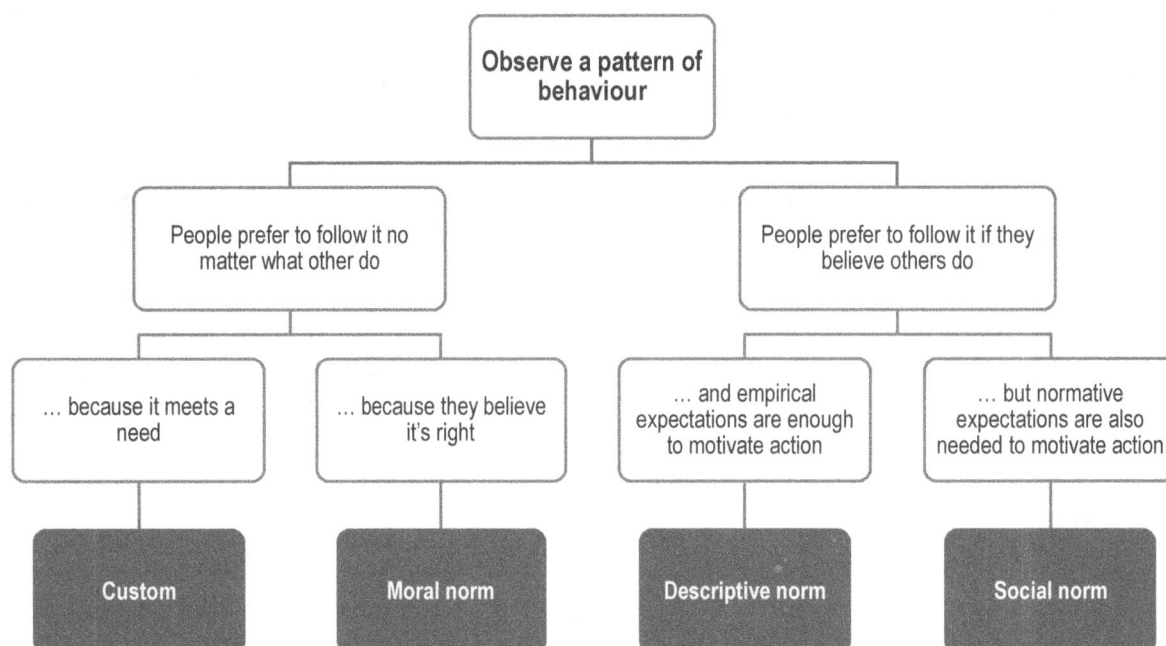

Source: Bicchieri and Penn Social Norms Training and Consulting Group, 2015, (Bicchieri, 2017[24]).

The existence of social norms within a given SAI could generate cultures that reinforce specific behaviours that in turn may unconsciously influence judgement and the work of the auditors. In a sense, they are a kind of social desirability bias. For example, independent from an auditor's training or his or her convictions about what auditors in general should do, this auditor may end up conforming to such a social norm prevalent in the unit or the SAI he or she is working in.

Such behavioural pattern that are conditional on others could explain the way auditors carry out their work, draft their findings and could affect the quantity of findings and recommendations. Auditors, for instance, may aim to find many observations or to provide very technical descriptions or justifications in the reports, if they believe that their superiors or colleagues expect such behaviour, because they see it, in the internal culture, as the typical product to be expected of a skilled and productive auditor. Following the social norm then becomes the best response to the given expectations, as it is likely to be rewarded (formally or informally). In turn, superiors or colleagues may perceive as incompetent or lazy an auditor that decides to start writing short reports in plain language and with concise recommendations.

As a consequence, such social dynamics influencing auditors' behaviours could lead to audit reports that are more tailored towards internal needs in terms of the auditor's career (performance evaluations, visibility or approval by colleagues and supervisors), than towards the need of the auditees. Again, this could undermine the relevance of the audit reports for the auditees and thus their uptake.

Auditees too are subject to behavioural barriers and biases

The auditee too may be subject to biases when receiving the audit results that can undermine their uptake. For example, people tend to see flaws in others more easily than in themselves and auditees may have difficulties to accept that errors have been committed by them or that doing things differently could improve their management. In addition, if the first perception or association of the auditing process or the audit report is negative, it is likely that everything related to the audit will be perceived negatively as well (anchoring effect) and trigger counter-reactions. This, in turn, may affect the follow-up of observations or the uptake of the recommendations. Finally, a study carried out in Norway shows that there may be effects related to the seniority of the audited public managers. In the Norwegian context, where the study has been carried out, high-ranking public servants seem to be less positive towards performance audits than are lower-ranking civil servants (Reichborn-Kjennerud, 2013[27]). Such a negative attitude may also imply that they are more inclined to reject findings included in the audit reports. At the same time, senior managers are usually the receivers of the audit reports.

Auditees may also perceive audit reports as unfair. As mentioned previously, audit criteria can help in guiding objectivity, but the criteria or their application can be perceived as unfair too. In turn, perceived fairness matters significantly. Findings from behavioural and social neurosciences suggest that experiencing unfair, exclusionary treatment can trigger reactions in the brain that are similar to experiencing pain (Eisenberger, Lieberman and Williams, 2003[28]). In addition, evidence suggest that subjective judgments of the fairness of outcomes are less important psychologically than subjective judgments of the fairness of process (Lind and Tyler, 1988[29]; Lind et al., 1993[30]; Walker et al., 1974[31]; Tyler, 2006[32]). Based on such findings, it is worth considering that by designing and administering regulations taking into account perceived fairness, governments can minimise experiences that citizens perceive as unfair. This, in turn, makes it more likely that they accept and comply with rules and decisions, feel included and trust their government (Lind and Arndt, 2016[33]).

Similar considerations apply to auditing processes too. If auditees perceive that they have been treated unfair – whether justified or not – they will be less likely to trust the auditors and the auditing process, they will unconsciously find justifications against the auditors and their findings and may therefore be less likely to follow or comply with the audit findings and recommendations.

Audit reports may fail to motivate auditees

Audit reports and recommendations may also fail to motivate auditees in implementing recommendations. As noted by the European Court of Auditors, audit reports tend to have an impersonal tone and can inadvertently distance the reader from the findings and observations (European Court of Auditors, 2013[34]). In part, this tone may be due to the deeply rooted strive for independence and objectivity within the audit profession.

Lack of motivation may also result from unclear responsibilities allowing public managers to rationalise inaction by refusing to see or to accept own responsibility, especially if non-compliance does not trigger any consequences. As such, recommendations should clearly address a specific group or office to avoid the diffusion of responsibility. A related problem is the tendency that some auditors may avoid providing definitive statements: *it appears that, it seems that, may have*. Such language may be needed in the absence of definitive criteria that requires auditees to take specific actions; however, it can also suggest that recommendations are simply suggestions, thereby and, again, promoting inaction.

Furthermore, some audit findings are typically phrased as observations stating, for example, incompliance with a regulation or procedure. Such observations, if they do not include guidance with respect to corrective actions or do not clearly show the auditee the rationale for addressing the observation, may not trigger the desired behaviour. However, as emphasised also in a recent EUROSAI report, SAIs should avoid putting themselves in a situation where they have to audit solutions that they have proposed themselves. Therefore, to strike a balance between helping auditees and avoiding such complications, recommendations could be formulated in a style where they describe *what* the auditee should do, and not *how* they should do it (EUROSAI, 2021[16]).

Finally, aggressive monitoring and scrutiny could negatively affect the intrinsic motivation of public managers to address audit observations and implement recommendations. Indeed, the introduction of a control mechanism or aggressive monitoring is a signal of distrust (OECD, 2018[7]). Overly strict control has been shown to significantly reduce the efforts of the person being controlled (Falk and Kosfeld, 2006[35]). It forces people to provide only the minimum effort necessary to pass the control, but removes the element of positive reciprocity: employees subject to controls might feel less obliged to deliver (Lambsdorff, 2015[36]; OECD, 2018[7]). Therefore, SAIs should strike the right balance between promoting compliance through intrinsic motivation and through control and monitoring when following up on audit reports.

Auditees' attention is limited

People's attention is limited and is easily distracted. Following-up with audit reports compete with other tasks of the public managers in the audited entities. Those responsible for implementing the corrective actions or considering and implementing the audit recommendations may simply be over-burdened by the workload and may fail to understand the relevance of the audit reports. Especially compliance audits, while necessary and relevant, may lead public managers to seek formal compliance only and to ensure that they have "ticked the right boxes". This approach is very human, as it minimises stress and effort given the workload created by the audit, but is contrary to good practices outlined in the OECD's Recommendation on Public Integrity and other international standards and is unlikely to drive real change.

Finally, when processes are too complicated, audit reports are too long, contain too much recommendations or there is in general too much information, auditees may experience decision fatigue from weighing too many inputs. This can result in public managers making the wrong choice, selecting the wrong priorities or deferring the choice all together. Over-burden may also generate or intensify an already negative attitude towards the work created through audits. In Norway for instance, a study found that officials most exposed to auditing were, in general, more negative towards it (Reichborn-Kjennerud, 2013[27]).

References

Avis, E., C. Ferraz and F. Finan (2018), "Do government audits reduce corruption? Estimating the impacts of exposing corrupt politicians", *Journal of Political Economy*, Vol. 126/5, pp. 1912-1964, https://doi.org/10.1086/699209. [18]

Bazerman, M., D. Moore and G. Loewenstein (2002), *Why good accountants do bad audits*. [21]

Bicchieri, C. (2017), *Norms in the wild: How to diagnose, measure, and change social norms*, https://doi.org/10.1093/acprof:oso/9780190622046.001.0001. [24]

Bicchieri, C. (2005), *The grammar of society: The nature and dynamics of social norms*, https://doi.org/10.1017/CBO9780511616037. [23]

Bicchieri, C., J. Lindemans and T. Jiang (2014), "A structured approach to a diagnostic of collective practices", *Frontiers in Psychology*, Vol. 5, https://doi.org/10.3389/fpsyg.2014.01418. [25]

Desmedt, E. et al. (2017), "Impact of performance audit on the administration: A belgian study (2005-2010)", *Managerial Auditing Journal*, Vol. 32/3, pp. 251-275, https://doi.org/10.1108/MAJ-04-2016-1368. [13]

Desmedt, E. and V. Pattyn (2015), *De impact van de performance audits van het Rekenhof. Survey bij ambtenaren van de federale overheid*, Versie Aanvaard Voor Publicatie in VTOM, Vlaams Tijdschrift Voor Overheidsmanagement, No. 7. 103-120. [15]

Eisenberger, N., M. Lieberman and K. Williams (2003), "Does rejection hurt? An fMRI study of social exclusion", *Science*, Vol. 302/5643, pp. 290-292, https://doi.org/10.1126/science.1089134. [28]

European Court of Auditors (2013), *Report-writing guideline*. [34]

EUROSAI (2021), *Follow-up of the implementation of audit recommendations: Best practices guide, issued by the project group*, European Organisation of Supreme Audit Institutions (EUROSAI). [16]

Falk, A. and M. Kosfeld (2006), "The Hidden Costs of Control", *American Economic Review*, Vol. 96/5, pp. 1611-1630. [35]

Ferraz, C. and F. Finan (2008), "Exposing corrupt politicians: The effects of Brazil's publicly released audits on electoral outcomes", *The Quarterly Journal of Economics* May, pp. 703-745, http://papers.ssrn.com/sol3/papers.cfm?abstract_id=997867 (accessed on 30 December 2014). [17]

IDI (2021), *Facilitating Audit Impact (FAI) Strategy*, INTOSAI Development Initiative, Oslo, https://idi.no/elibrary/relevant-sais/fai/1408-facilitating-audit-impact-fai-strategy/file (accessed on 12 April 2022). [3]

INTOSAI (2019), *Code of Ethics - International Standards of Supreme Audit Institutions ISSAI 130*, International Organisation of Supreme Audit Institutions, Vienna, https://www.issai.org/pronouncements/issai-130-code-of-ethics/ (accessed on 5 May 2021). [19]

INTOSAI (2019), *INTOSAI-P 12 The Value and Benefits of Supreme Audit Institutions: Making a difference to the lives of citizens*, AuditInternational Organisation of Supreme Audit Institutions (INTOSAI). [1]

INTOSAI (2019), *ISSAI 100 Fundamental Principles of Public-Sector Auditing*, International Organisation of Supreme Audit Institutions (INTOSAI), https://www.issai.org/pronouncements/issai-100-fundamental-principles-of-public-sector-auditing/ (accessed on 17 May 2021). [20]

INTOSAI (2010), *How to increase the use and impact of audit reports: A guide for Supreme Audit Institutions*, INTOSAI Capacity Building Committee, https://iniciativatpa.org/wp-content/uploads/2014/05/Increase-impact-of-audit-reports.pdf (accessed on 28 September 2020). [2]

Kassin, S., I. Dror and J. Kukucka (2013), "The forensic confirmation bias: Problems, perspectives, and proposed solutions", *Journal of Applied Research in Memory and Cognition*, Vol. 2/1, pp. 42-52, https://doi.org/10.1016/j.jarmac.2013.01.001. [10]

Kida, T. (1984), *The Impact of Hypothesis-Testing Strategies on Auditors' Use of Judgment Data*. [8]

Kinney, W. and W. Uecker (1982), *Mitigating the Consequences of Anchoring in Auditor Judgments*, https://www.jstor.org/stable/246739. [9]

Lambsdorff, J. (2015), "Preventing corruption by promoting trust – insights from behavioral science", *Passauer Diskussionspapiere*, No. V-69-15, Universität Passau, Passau, https://doi.org/10.13140/RG.2.1.3563.4006. [36]

Lind, E. and C. Arndt (2016), "Perceived Fairness and Regulatory Policy: A Behavioural Science Perspective on Government-Citizen Interactions", *OECD Regulatory Policy Working Papers*, No. 6, OECD Publishing, Paris, https://doi.org/10.1787/1629d397-en. [33]

Lind, E. et al. (1993), "Individual and Corporate Dispute Resolution: Using Procedural Fairness as a Decision Heuristic", *Administrative Science Quarterly*, Vol. 38/2, p. 224, https://doi.org/10.2307/2393412. [30]

Lind, E. and T. Tyler (1988), *The Social Psychology of Procedural Justice*, Springer US, Boston, MA, https://doi.org/10.1007/978-1-4899-2115-4. [29]

OECD (2019), *Tools and Ethics for Applied Behavioural Insights: The BASIC Toolkit*, OECD Publishing, Paris, https://doi.org/10.1787/9ea76a8f-en. [6]

OECD (2018), *Behavioural Insights for Public Integrity: Harnessing the Human Factor to Counter Corruption*, OECD Public Governance Reviews, OECD Publishing, Paris, https://doi.org/10.1787/9789264297067-en. [7]

OECD (2017), *Behavioural Insights and Public Policy: Lessons from Around the World*, OECD Publishing, Paris, https://doi.org/10.1787/9789264270480-en. [11]

OECD (2016), *Progress in Chile's Supreme Audit Institution: Reforms, Outreach and Impact*, OECD Public Governance Reviews, OECD Publishing, Paris, https://doi.org/10.1787/9789264250635-en. [5]

OECD (2016), *Supreme Audit Institutions and Good Governance: Oversight, Insight and Foresight*, OECD Public Governance Reviews, OECD Publishing, Paris, https://doi.org/10.1787/9789264263871-en. [12]

OECD (2014), *Chile's Supreme Audit Institution: Enhancing Strategic Agility and Public Trust*, OECD Public Governance Reviews, OECD Publishing, Paris, https://doi.org/10.1787/9789264207561-en. [4]

Pennington, R., J. Schafer and R. Pinsker (2017), "Do Auditor Advocacy Attitudes Impede Audit Objectivity?", *Journal of Accounting, Auditing & Finance*, Vol. 32/1, pp. 136-151, https://doi.org/10.1177/0148558X16641862. [22]

Reichborn-Kjennerud, K. (2013), "Resistance to Control—Norwegian Ministries' and Agencies' Reactions to Performance Audit", *Public Organization Review*, Vol. 15/1, pp. 17-32, https://doi.org/10.1007/s11115-013-0247-6. [27]

Tyler, T. (2006), *Why People Obey the Law*, Princeton University Press, Princeton. [32]

Van Loocke, E. and V. Put (2011), *The Impact of Performance Audits: A Review of the Existing Evidence*, Edward Elgar Publishing, https://doi.org/10.4337/9780857931801.00016. [14]

Walker, L. et al. (1974), "Reactions of Participants and Observers to Modes of Adjudication1", *Journal of Applied Social Psychology*, Vol. 4/4, pp. 295-310, https://doi.org/10.1111/j.1559-1816.1974.tb02601.x. [31]

Yamin et al. (2019), "Using Social Norms to Change Behavior and Increase Sustainability in the Real World: A Systematic Review of the Literature", *Sustainability*, Vol. 11/20, p. 5847, https://doi.org/10.3390/su11205847. [26]

Note

[1] Note that Brazil's Office of Comptroller-General (CGU) is responsible for internal audits, however. Brazil's SAI is the Federal Court of Accounts (Tribunal de Contas da União, TCU).

2 Main challenges to the follow-up of audit reports in Chile

This chapter presents the current follow-up process to audit reports in Chile as well as the main challenges that reduce the likelihood that auditees will address audit observations. In Chile, these challenges are mainly related to the quantity of audit observations, perceptions of unfairness, communication as well as capacity constraints. These challenges are, amongst others, leading to decision fatigue and affecting the motivation of auditees and their attitude towards audit in general.

The follow-up process to external audit reports in Chile

To understand how behavioural insights could help improving the implementation rate of audit observations in Chile, some background information is necessary. The inductive approach of applying behavioural insights implies that the proposed strategies to address identified issues, proposed in Chapter 3, need to be grounded in a thorough understanding of the given context. To provide the relevant background, this section briefly reviews the scope of external audits in Chile, the follow-up process to audit reports and the main actors involved in this process.

The mandate for external audit in Chile is focusing on compliance audits

In Chile, the audit reports produced by the Comptroller General of the Republic (*Contraloría General de la República*, CGR) currently focus on legal compliance. The reports contain observations (*observaciones*) with respect to non-compliance with regulations or procedures. The audited services should correct these observations to ensure compliance. CGR audit reports usually only describe the finding, not avenues for taking corrective actions. Since 2014, efforts have been made by the CGR to guide auditors in providing guidance to auditees on what actions could be taken to respond to the observations and the auditors may include suggestions for corrective actions (Service Order 30 of 2014). Due care must be taken, of course, to not co-administrate. Nonetheless, interviews with auditees indicated that they sometimes would welcome more guidance to ensure the correct follow-up.

Similar to other countries in Latin America (Figure 2.1), the CGR in Chile currently does not have a mandate to conduct performance audits in Chile (OECD, 2020[1]). Performance audits could lead to audit recommendations, where the value added to public management is easier to see for heads of services and public managers. Indeed, SAIs are using performance audits to provide valuable insights into complex problems and risks, such as modernising outdated financial regulatory systems and protecting public safety (OECD, 2020[1]).

There are discussions to broaden CGR's mandate to include performance audits. In fact, since 2019 the CGR has carried out 3E audits (Efficiency, effectiveness and economy), which, although based on legal compliance, have a more performance-oriented approach. In 2020, the CGR also has implemented a Financial Audit Department that has performed Financial Audits over the last years. However, these are still new developments and are not yet widely applied. In fact, traditionally, the mandate of the CGR in Chile excludes auditing the "merit" of political or administrative decisions and considers that the verification and assessment of whether policy objectives and goals have been achieved is a mandate of the public administration, not of the CGR. Nonetheless, as highlighted in the OECD Review of Chile's SAI, performance auditing does not need to question the merit of intentions and decisions; instead, it may focus on examining possible shortcomings in organisation, management and support and Chile could consider continue moving in this direction (OECD, 2014[2]). Of course, compliance audits will continue to play an important role in the future.

Figure 2.1. SAI mandate for performance audits in Latin America, 2019

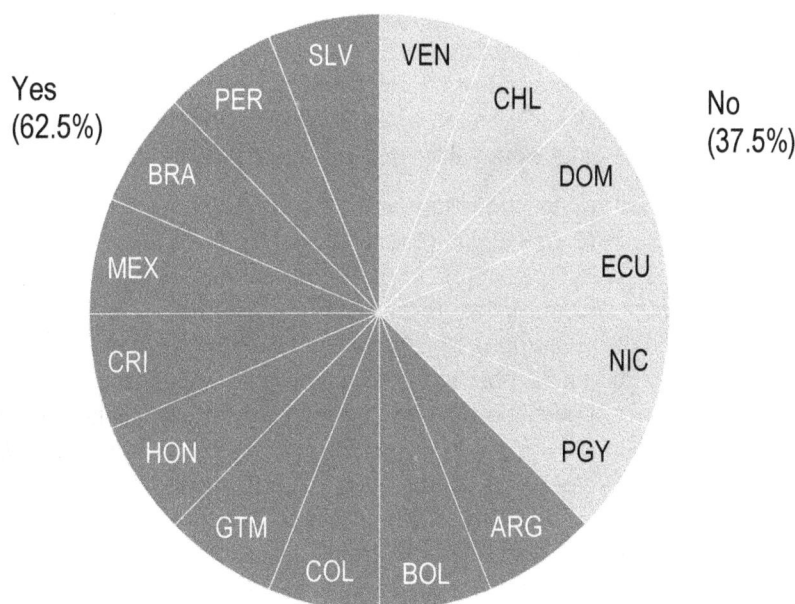

Note: The original survey question is: "What type of audits (compliance, financial, or performance) has the Supreme Audit Institution (SAI) conducted and made available to the public?" The graphs above counted as "Yes" all countries scoring a 100, meaning the countries conduct all three type of audits, and as "No" countries score 67 or 33, meaning the countries conduct at least one or two of the types of audits. The value for Colombia has been corrected to "yes" reflecting that the Office of the Comptroller General of the Republic of Colombia is allowed to conduct performance audits (OECD, 2021[3]).

Source: International Budget Partnership, Open Budget Survey 2019.

The process to follow-up on audit reports has been reviewed and has improved over the past years

The process through which the CGR follows up on audit reports to monitor and increase the uptake of the audit observations has changed and improved significantly over the last decade. Until 2012, the follow-up to previous audit reports was carried out when the CGR auditors visited the same entity for a new audit. However, given that the CGR's coverage includes close to 4 000 audited services (*servicios*) at both national and municipal level, it was very difficult for the CGR to visit an entity again in the short term. Auditors in the field then had to balance follow-up work with audit planning and audit execution. As a consequence, the follow-up processes were many times simply not carried out or not carried out in a timely manner, with the consequence that it was difficult for the CGR to keep track of and measure the uptake of the audit observations.

In 2012, the CGR created audit follow-up units (*Unidades de Seguimiento*) to ensure that auditees respond to observations and implement corrective measures (CGR Resolution 06920/2011). The audit follow-up units, which are independent from the auditing teams, started to be implemented in February 2012. The CGR's National Follow-up Co-ordination Unit (*Coordinación Nacional de Seguimiento*) leads and co-ordinates the audit follow-up units and develops manuals and technical guides to support the follow-up process. Together, the National Follow-up Co-ordination Unit and the audit follow-up units allowed to make a broader and timelier verification of the compliance with the audit observations provided by the CGR, while generating relevant information about the process and its results.

In 2014, the OECD Review of the CGR found that stakeholders still perceive the work of the CGR as focusing mainly on detecting errors and on the legality of acts. To improve its impact, the OECD Review recommended broadening the scope of the information it provides, the methods of delivering this information and the working with the recipient audience. The Review further recommended to co-operate with public institutions, including the internal audit structure in Chile, and in particular the Council of Government's General Internal Auditors (*Consejo de Auditoría Interna General de Gobierno*, CAIGG), to ensure efficiency and effectiveness of its work while maintaining its independence (OECD, 2014[2]).

Two years later, the survey carried out for the follow-up of the OECD Review documented progress and showed that both CGR officials and external stakeholders recognised the efforts of the CGR towards better engaging its various audiences (OECD, 2016[4]). Improvements have also been made in the system through which the CGR monitors and compiles its audit findings. In particular, as of 2014, the CGR's Integrated System for Audit Control (*Sistema Integrado para el Control de Auditorias*, SICA) began to be used. The SICA allows recording a large amount of information on monitoring results. This tool, together with the audit follow-up units, made it possible to verify more timely the compliance with the observations made by the CGR. The information also feeds the planning processes for future audits. The SICA also enables the CGR to process and synthesise audit findings to generate rankings of public sector entities and municipalities. These ranking take into account addressed observations and engaged disciplinary proceedings. This reflects a move from the act of monitoring audit reports to monitoring observations more broadly. Currently, observations remain active until corrected, regardless of their date or association to any individual audit (OECD, 2016[4]). The SICA was updated in 2021 with the objective to make it more user-friendly.

In 2016 the CGR created the Compliance Support Programme (*Programa de Apoyo al Cumplimiento*, PAC) to support the implementation of observations through the audit follow-up units. The programme provides methodological tools to public entities to help them analyse the problems detected in the audits and define a work plan that allows to overcome these problems and to prevent repeating the same errors in the future.

In addition, in 2018 the responsibility for monitoring the implementation of observations of lower levels of complexity was transferred to the internal control officers of the audited services (Official Letter 14.100). Indeed, observations are being classified according to their complexity:

- highly complex and complex observations, that may compromise administrative, civil or criminal responsibility of the officials involved
- moderately complex and slightly complex observations, that do not entail administrative, civil or criminal responsibility of the officials involved.

These changes with respect to the monitoring responsibility allowed to reduce the workload of the CGR's audit follow-up units, thereby improving their capacity to follow-up the overall implementation process and to focus on observations of higher complexity and higher impact. In addition, by involving the internal audit units, the changes allowed a better alignment and co-operation between internal and external audit functions. In 2018, the CGR launched an online system to support public entities in monitoring the follow-up of observations by streamlining the processes and facilitating the reporting. The system also allows the CGR to follow-up the work plans elaborated together with the audited services participating in the PAC. Public entities were trained about how to use this system to ensure a successful implementation of this platform.

Figure 2.2 summarises the steps of the audit follow-up process that aims at increasing the uptake of audit reports. The CGR reports the observations that require follow-up via the audit report including deadlines to address them. The individual responsible for internal audit in the audited entity (i.e. the Internal Auditor or, in municipalities, the Director of Internal Control) receives a notification per e-mail, organises a work team of public managers in the concerned areas of the entity. Through the online system, the Internal Auditor or Director of Internal Control is able to assign tasks and to manage and follow-up the implementation of the corrective measures. The system also generates automatically alerts when deadlines are approaching. Once public managers have implemented the corrective measures, they can upload the information into the system. The Internal Auditor or Director of Internal Control reviews this information and either reports the recommendation as addressed (for observations of lower complexity levels) or sends the information to the CGR through the SICA (for observations of higher levels of complexity). In the latter case, the CGR reviews the information provided and closes the monitoring process if the auditee took the necessary corrective measures. Otherwise, the CGR maintains the observations. In addition to reviewing the information entered into the system, if necessary, the follow-up units can also make field visits to the audited services.

Figure 2.2. The CGR's audit follow-up processes

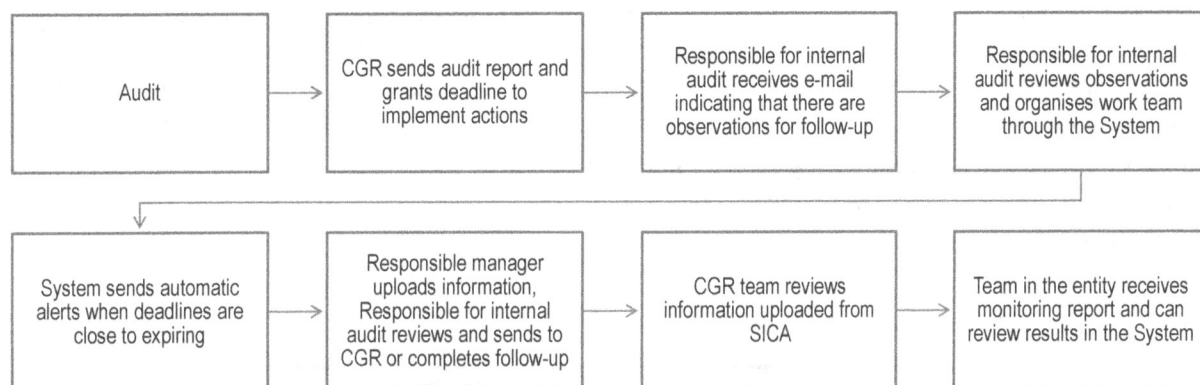

Source: Elaborated based on information provided by the CGR Chile.

The actors involved in the audit and the audit follow-up process

The behavioural perspective looks at the process from the perspective of the involved individuals. Their behaviour needs to be understood and potentially targeted to improve the uptake of audit observations in the Chilean context.

At the level of the CGR, these individuals are:

- The auditors of the CGR in charge of conducting and supervising the audits (Audit Executive and audit teams) are in direct contact with the audited service and communicate with the Internal Auditors or Directors of Internal Control as well as, to a lesser degree, with public managers. They carry out the audit that leads to the observations issued to the service and are responsible for drafting the reports. Supervisors are in charge of several audit teams and play an important role in shaping the auditing process.
- The staff in CGR's Technical Planning Secretariat (*Secretaría Técnica de Planificación*) and in the regional units of the CGR are in charge of notifying auditees of an upcoming audit.
- The audit follow-up teams of the CGR at central and at regional level and the National Follow-up Co-ordination Unit within the CGR monitor and follow-up the audit reports. They communicate with and provide guidance and support to the services on addressing the observations.

At the level of the audited services, the key actors in Chile are:

- The responsible for internal audit (the Internal Auditor at national level or the Director of Internal Control at municipal level) plays a key role, as they are the transmission belt between the CGR, the Head of the service and the public managers of the entity.

- The Head of the service (designated Minister, Director or similar at national level, and elected Mayor at municipal level) have the ultimate responsibility for the actions taken in their service. They respond to political incentives if appointed or electoral incentives if elected.
- The heads of units in the audited services (public managers) that have been subject to the audits by the CGR are those who, in the end, implement (or not) the recommendations issued by the CGR in their area of responsibilities.

The uptake of audit observations in Chile

Thanks to the improvements achieved by the CGR over the past years, the audit-follow up processes were able to evidence that, on average over the period 2015-2020, only 50% of the observations were being corrected. As the CGR is carrying out compliance audits, this number appears to be relatively low and have triggered the interest of the CGR in improving the uptake. The CGR shared the consolidated data on observations resulting from the audit monitoring processes since 2015 with the OECD. Two tables summarise the information.

Table 2.1 shows that between 2015 and 2020, the CGR issued 57 613 observations. The average number of observations was of 9 938 observations per year. All observations are distributed over 1 894 services that were audited during this period.

Table 2.1. Quantity of observations, 2015-2020

Year	Total observations
2015	7 950
2016	9 399
2017	10 608
2018	11 058
2019	10 679
2020	7 919
Total	**57 613**

Source: CGR, calculations OECD.

In turn, Table 2.2 shows that there is a large amount of data points in the dataset without information concerning the status of the follow-up to the observations. According to the CGR, most of the observations without information correspond to observations that have not been followed-up actively, either by the audited service in the case of less complex observations, or by the CGR in complex cases. Some of the observations that have been classified as "Not followed-up" include observations that did not correspond or were it was untimely to follow up on the matter. Overall, the data shows that 46 183 observations have been followed up either by the CGR or by the Internal Auditors or the Directors of Internal Control of the audited services, of which 23 124 have been corrected during this period. Therefore, according to the available data, approximately 50 % of observations that have been subject to follow-up monitoring were not corrected.

Table 2.2. Status of the observations according to their follow-up and uptake, 2015-2020

Status	Without information	Active (Maintained/Not addressed)	Corrected (Addressed)	Total general
Followed-up	1 023	22 036	**23 124**	**46 183**
Not followed-up	6 759	2 926	1 745	11 430
Total general	7 782	24 962	24 869	57 613

Source: CGR, calculations OECD.

Principal challenges explaining the uptake of audit observations in Chile

The quantitative and qualitative research conducted by the OECD evidenced underlying challenges, which create an environment that influences the behaviours, attitudes and perceptions of the auditors and auditees. Sometimes, auditees may have valid reasons to disagree with observations in the audit reports. However, as discussed in Chapter 1 and summarised in Figure 2.3, disagreement with observations or the attitude towards them is not always triggered by rational criteria only.

Figure 2.3. Potential behavioural factors undermining the uptake of audit recommendations

Auditing is principally a matter of human judgement	Auditors are influenced by social norms	Auditees too are subject to behavioural barriers and biases	Audit reports may fail to motivate auditees	Auditees attention is limited
• Cognitive biases (e.g. confirmation bias) can undermine auditors' professional judgement – this can be perceived by the auditees and delegitimise the recommendations	• Informal norms within the SAIs may provide incentives to tailor reports following internal dynamics and not considering the auditee's needs	• Cognitive biases and perceptions of the auditees can undermine their acceptance of the audit reports • Perceived unfairness in the auditing process may undermine the auditees' inclination to trust the auditors, to accept the findings and implement the recommendations	• Audit recommendations, if not presented adequately or failing to assign clear responsibilities, may fail to motivate public managers to act or allow for diffusion of responsibility • Aggressive monitoring or follow-up can undermine the intrinsic motivation of auditees	• Overly complex or too many observations or too much information may cause decision fatigue, a negative attitude towards audit or the ability to see the relevance of the audit reports

The qualitative analysis carried out in Chile confirmed several of the potential underlying behavioural barriers and biases suggested in Chapter 1. In particular, the following three challenges contribute to explain the rate of implementation of the observations included in the audit reports in Chile and will be discussed in more detail in the following subsections:

1. The quantity of observations undermines their implementation and can trigger decision fatigue and a negative attitude towards audit in general.

2. Perception of unfairness by auditees and weaknesses in communication between auditors and auditees can undermine the willingness to address audit findings.

3. Heads of services and public management in the audited services show low levels of interest, ownership and motivation with respect to addressing the audit results.

The quantity of observations undermines their implementation and can trigger decision fatigue and a negative attitude towards audit in general

A major and consistent finding evidenced by the interviews with different stakeholders relates to the quantity of the audit observations. Too many observations are causing attention bias. In part, the legalistic nature of the compliance audits carried out by the CGR inherently may tend to lead to a higher number of observations, as it is difficult to leave out even minor legal issues and because there is a challenge to assess the relevance of observations related to non-compliance with regulations or procedures. However, the quantity of detailed observations makes it difficult for auditees to see the bigger picture. While the characterisation of observations according to their complexity helps to classify the observations and therefore could contribute to make the list of observations more "digestible" to auditees, a recurrent reason for the backlog in addressing observations mentioned by stakeholders still was related to the quantity of observations, which is exacerbated by capacity constraints.

A high concentration of observations in certain services may affect the uptake of audit reports

The data provided by the CGR indicates a relatively high level of saturation of some audited services when it comes to observations. The average number of observations per audit report that were included in the follow-up process during the period between 2015 and 2020 was of approximately 5, with a standard deviation of 7.30, which shows that there are significant differences between audit reports. Likewise, the average number of total observations included in the follow-up process per audited service in the period analysed was 28. In the available dataset, the entity with the most observations had 371 observations, while many had only one observation. On average, approximately 25% of the audited services received more than 30 observations, accumulating 69% of the total observations. This shows a relatively high level of concentration of observations on a small group of audited services. As one official mentioned in the interview: "*Mentally, a high number of observations is difficult to digest… it is better to have fewer than too many observations.*"

This concentration creates significant work to the internal audit areas of these services in addition to the work defined in their annual internal audit plan. Despite the fact that the 592 services, which concentrate most of the observations, are responsible for 74.4% of the recommendations corrected, they are at the same time responsible for 79% of those which have not been corrected. Significantly, 78.6% of the observations that have not been addressed, have been issued to the entities already showing the highest concentration of observations. Therefore, the higher the number of audits, the lower the percentage of uptake of observations. This seems again to indicate a relatively high burden of work related to the follow up and implementation of the audit observations and could contribute, amongst other factors, to explain the low levels of implementation. Table 2.3 evidences the fact that the 20 municipal services and the 20 non-municipal services exhibiting the highest numbers of observations are respectively responsible for 9.9% and 8.3% of the number of unaddressed observations. In other words, around 2% of the services (40 out of 1931) are alone accounting for 18.2% of the unaddressed observations.

Table 2.3. Share of unaddressed observations by the most congested services

Share of the 20 most congested municipal services	
No. of unaddressed observations	Share
2 189	9.9%
Share of the 20 most congested non-municipal services	
No. of unaddressed observations	Share
1 817	8.3%

Source: CGR, calculations OECD.

According to the CGR, two factors could explain the concentration of observations in a reduced number of services. First, some services could be more involved in interacting directly with citizens and may therefore be more prone to complaints and reports by the users of these services. However, the available data does not allow verifying this. Second, and more importantly, according to the CGR, services with a higher level of risk are more likely to be audited because audit plans are informed by risk analysis. In turn, the higher the number of audits, the higher the number of observations. As such, there could be a vicious cycle leading to a "concentration trap" of audit observations in certain services. Indeed, given that the CGR uses the non-implementation of the required corrective actions as an indicator to rank the services and to inform the audit plans, the saturation of observations could generate a low implementation rate, which in turn makes the services even more susceptible to new audits, leading to even more observations.

Capacity constraints and weaknesses at the level of services could exacerbate this vicious cycle. Services with weak capacities may also be particular vulnerable to errors, mismanagement and imply higher risks of fraud and corruption. Therefore, these entities may be subject to more audits and thus more observations, stretching the capacity constraints even further. In particular, weaknesses in the internal control system may lead to more observations. In one interview, an internal auditor mentioned that "quite a few observations could have been prevented through a better internal control system." In turn, it was reported that entities that are well staffed tend to have higher compliance rates with observations within the stipulated deadlines and are also the entities that most likely are to contest the criteria used and observations issued in the reports.

Interviews indicate that these findings may be particularly relevant for some municipalities. In fact, data shows that municipalities have the lowest degree of uptake of observations. During the interviews, it was mentioned that small municipalities often have not yet adapted to new challenges to public management and that they suffer from high staff rotation and low technical capacities. These capacity constraints can lead to errors in processes and management and later to audit observations and a higher probability of being audited again. In turn, a high probability of being audited or having been audited several times causes a greater negative predisposition towards external control. This may unconsciously influence the priority public managers give to take corrective actions.

The interviews conducted confirm that a large number of observations in some services both at national and municipal level generates saturation especially in the internal control area. This accumulation and the impression of being trapped in a high level of observations could trigger or reinforce adverse reactions to the auditing process and the reports in the audited services. In some services, staff of the internal audit areas are reportedly dedicated full time to answering to the observations issued by the CGR and to following up internally that these observations are being addressed by public managers. Interviews emphasised that the staff and resources dedicated to reacting to the observations are missing to carry out internal audit work that could lead to preventing future observations and achieve other improvements.

Amongst internal audit areas, there is a feeling of having to neglect "own" work to carry out work created by the CGR, while at the same time feeling that the CGR does not recognise enough the efforts they undertake. Of course, services with many observations have to dedicate significant efforts and resources to follow them up and to take corrective actions. Despite dedicating staff and resources exclusively to following-up and responding to the CGR observations, auditees indicated that in many cases, it is not possible for them to deal with all observations on time (see also below). Overall, some internal audit areas expressed during the interviews that they sometimes feel left alone with the burden imposed by the audit reports. They stated to welcome more continuous support and guidance by the CGR; also outside the Compliance Support Programme (PAC).

Misunderstandings and communication failures can lead to include observations in audit reports that could have been avoided

Communication can affect the quantity of observations. Interviews reported that poor communication by auditors during the audit or the lack of clarity in what the auditor expects from the public managers sometimes leads to misunderstandings. For example, the public manager may provide information or responses that are not the ones expected by the auditor. This, in turn may lead to observations that could have been avoided by a better communication on the spot.

Moreover, this lack of communication and feedback perceived by auditees during or right after the auditing process can bring along additional undesired effects. For instance, when receiving the pre-report, where the auditees "discover" the audit findings for the first time, public managers have expressed to feel frustrated when reading observations that, according to them, could have been addressed easily during the audit if the communication with the auditors would have been more open and fluid. Similarly, confirming the concern expressed by public managers, the Directors of Internal Control and Internal Auditors reported that unnecessary stress is caused because some observations are based on issues that could have been resolved before they were issued, if they would have been consulted.

This situation creates frustration, exacerbated by the fact that the interaction between internal audit areas and the CGR takes place mainly after the CGR issued the audit report. This creates a sense of powerlessness. Auditees spend time and effort on addressing observations that could have been avoided or on which there is a disagreement that could have been raised and clarified earlier. Overall, interviews indicate that internal audit areas are not sufficiently and proactively involved and consulted during the audit process.

Informal norms within the CGR drive the behaviour of auditors towards including more observations and being strict about maintaining them

Auditors in Chile, as elsewhere, are guided by relevant laws and regulations as well as by professional standards and values. However, as human beings, their behaviour is also influenced by social norms that are not always aligned with the formal rules. The interviews conducted with both auditees and the CGR indeed found that there is to some degree an internal culture in the CGR that pressures auditors to include a large number of findings in the reports. Reportedly, a "good" auditor is an auditor able to detect many issues and thus observations.

This, in turn, not only contributes to the quantity of observations but also affects potentially their quality, as not all the observations may be relevant. In addition, at times, the auditors are reportedly also reluctant to "drop" observations in the face of new information presented by the auditees, since that could be considered as "soft" or not objective. Overall, this can cause discomfort in the auditees and make it difficult for them to focus on what really matters and is urgent.

The phenomenon seems to be related entirely to social norms that are shaping the organisational culture. It is important to emphasise that there is indeed no formal requirement in the CGR that sets incentives for such a behaviour by the auditors. One interview partner mentioned that there could be a generational aspect to the issue, as auditors that are more senior are more likely to have been exposed to a more "severe" approach to auditing. Younger auditors entering the CGR may be aware of a more modern, client-oriented approach to auditing, but are likely to adapt to the behaviour that is expected by them by more senior auditors and what they observe amongst colleagues.

Perception of unfairness by auditees and weaknesses in communication between auditors and auditees can undermine the willingness to address audit findings

Audit criteria are perceived to be unequally applied across the public administration, which can generate a sense of unfair treatment

Perceived unfairness in applying audit criteria can generate defiant reactions of auditees towards the audit reports as well as undermine their acceptance of audit findings and thus their willingness to take corrective actions. Interviews in Chile showed that public officials that have worked in different services and therefore have a certain comparative perspective, perceive or believe to have experienced that audit criteria are not the same everywhere and that audit processes are not sufficiently standardised. While the CGR has made important efforts to standardise audit criteria, it is also true that the context varies and that each audit process is different, which in turn may lead to the perception of unequal treatment.

For instance, according to the interviews conducted by the OECD, transversal audits of the same services across regions have reportedly led to different conclusions and therefore observations, which could indeed lead to the perception of an unequal use of audit criteria. In addition, reportedly, in some cases auditors write observations concerning an issue that has not been raised elsewhere in an otherwise identical process. Such a perception of "unfair" audits can contribute to creating a general sense of an unequal treatment by the CGR and trigger counterproductive reactions by the auditees, providing justifications to dismiss actually well founded observations.

Uncertainty with respect to the publication of the audit report and perceived tight and inflexible deadlines imposed by the CGR create stress and frustration

Auditees mentioned tight and inflexible deadlines several times during the interviews. The remarks concerned both deadlines for requests during the auditing and deadlines related to addressing the observations issued in the reports. First, public managers and internal auditors flagged that short deadlines for responding to requests from CGR auditors during the on-site audit activities may sometimes lead to unsatisfactory responses because of time pressure. Again, similar to – and in addition to – the lack of communication and feedback already mentioned above, public managers reported that the time pressure sometimes lead to observations that could have been avoided. Managers and internal audit staff reported that discovering this when receiving the pre-report was creating some level of frustration.

Second, auditees expressed that deadlines can be too short to respond with due care to some observations or that it may even be impossible to comply with some deadlines. It is relevant to note that the deadlines for taking corrective actions never exceed 60 working days, which may be more than enough time to address many observations, but indeed not enough to deal with others. Especially public managers perceive the deadlines for addressing the observations as not realistic or not adapted to the reality of the public administration. They reported that the deadlines do not take into account the nature of the activity related to the observations or the available capacities to address them. For example, they mentioned that some processes related to construction contracts or disciplinary proceedings may de facto take longer than the deadlines imposed by the CGR. In addition, responding to the audit observations sometimes may require a significant amount of internal co-ordination and/or internal requests for advisory or concepts from the legal department. Both internal co-ordination and internal legal requests can take time. In addition, interviews with public managers flagged that many management processes are dynamic and change over the course of the follow-up process so that deadlines are not achievable or require a large investment of time and resources.

These deadlines that are applied uniformly and are not flexible to adapt to the specific cases and circumstances, together with the time pressure coming along with deadlines that cannot be met, negatively affect the quality of the follow-up by auditees. This, in turn, may lead to new requests by the CGR, creating more pressure. As mentioned previously, public managers and internal audit areas face situations of attention bias and decision fatigue because of the amount of work and the responsibilities that comes along with the process of following up on audit observations. Coupled with the deadlines, the work can create stress, especially if meeting the deadline is impossible and may lead to leaving "normal" work undone, as significant part of resources have to be dedicated to responding to the CGR.

The frustration related to the deadlines for taking corrective actions are exacerbated by the fact that the time span between the on-site audit activities and the reception of the audit report can be long (often more than a year) and may vary significantly, making it virtually impossible to predict when the report will arrive. In addition, auditees perceive that the CGR does not announce with sufficient anticipation the audit report (or the pre-report, for that matter). Indeed, this uncertainty was emphasised by public managers and internal audit staff as it creates difficulties to plan follow-up and generates stress. Public managers reported that this uncertainty does not allow them to plan their time accordingly, with the result that the audit report sometimes coincides – and conflicts – with already planned activities.

The way audit reports are drafted and the relationship between auditor and auditee may nurture a negative attitude of the auditees towards the CGR and the observations

Misunderstandings and failures in communication may not only contribute to the quantity of the observations, as mentioned above, but also and in particular to their acceptance. Interviews indicated that especially heads of audited services and public managers sometimes lack an understanding of the standards and criteria used in the audits or are not able to correctly understand and assess the relevance of the observations. The technical and legal language of the audit reports, reinforced by the current social norm in the CGR described previously, may exacerbate this, making it at times difficult to understand for non-auditors or non-lawyers. In addition, the nature of the compliance reports may imply that the CGR does not dedicate sufficient space to give credit to auditees for progress and positive actions taken. In fact, more often than not, such a positive perspective is lacking entirely.

From a behavioural perspective, both aspects could generate fatigue and a negative attitude towards the audit reports. If the first impression of a report is negative, it is likely that everything that is associated with it will be perceived negatively as well. In particular, it may negatively frame the attitude towards the observations contained in the audit report making it less likely that auditees will handle them with due care.

On a more diffuse level, it was reported that the CGR often still generates fear amongst public managers and, consequently, sometimes aversion against auditing processes. While most interviewed auditees agreed that the CGR has improved and that efforts are being noted to come across less distant and severe, the CGR still seems to struggle in being perceived as a partner or as supporting management. Again, the social norms described above could undermine efforts by the CGR to improve the relation between auditors and auditees. While auditors of course have to maintain their independence and stay at arms-length from the auditees, the de facto severe attitude reportedly contributes to negative associations with audits and, as a consequence, with the audit reports and the observations.

Heads of services and public management in the audited services show low levels of interest, ownership and motivation with respect to addressing the audit results

Some interviews pointed out that heads of services and public managers of the audited areas often are not exhibiting strong levels of commitment, ownership and motivation in relation to the audit process and its results.

In part, this certainly could be explained by the fact that non-compliance with audit observations seldom leads to sanctions in Chile. In most cases, the CGR follow-up units simply assign a new deadline to the auditee to address the concerned observations. Only when audit observations are of high public visibility, when senior managers are involved or when there was a harm to public patrimony, failure to comply could lead to disciplinary procedures. However, in Chile, such sanctions are reportedly rather exceptional and even if applied, public officials perceive them as rather weak. On the one hand, the process usually takes a long time. On the other hand, the CGR can only propose the sanction, which needs to be ratified and applied by the public entity, where the sanction is often either lowered or completely dismissed. Consequently, interviews indicated that non-compliance comes along with little consequences and as such low risks for the responsible public managers.

However, beyond a lack of perceived pressure, interviews revealed other aspects that contribute to explain the low level of interest, ownership or motivation of auditees with respect to audit reports.

On the one hand, at the highest level, heads of service have to set priorities and cannot be involved in all operational details of management. While the heads of services are formally responsible for the corrective actions, many observations are arguably too technical to be interesting for them or are perceived as not relevant from a strategic perspective. Interviews emphasised that heads of services typically become interested in audit reports if these are politically relevant or if they seem to indicate corrupt practices in their entity that could affect their reputation, the reputation of the entity or could lead to potential sanctions. Nonetheless, even if it is reasonable that their interest focuses on strategic or high-level issues, the lack of leadership with respect to audit reports could signal within the entity that they are of low priority. Interviews also indicated that where there is a fluent and trust-based relationship between heads of services and internal auditors, the follow-up process of CGR audit report becomes easier. Then, public managers in the entity see that audit, whether internal or external, is taken seriously at the highest level.

On the other hand, at the level of public managers who are directly involved in or have the direct responsibility over the audited processes, similar aspects where highlighted during the interviews. First, public managers also perceive many observations as too legalistic or too technical. In addition, they may lack awareness concerning the benefits – for them – resulting from taking corrective actions.

Second, interviews emphasised that high levels of staff rotation may affect the follow-up of audit reports by public managers. While more acute at municipal level, this can also be observed at the central level and is exacerbated by the fact that many public employees are contracted for a year, with possible extension ("*contrata*" regime), or contracting for specific services that in theory should not be maintained over time ("*honorarios*" regime) (Dirección de Presupuestos, 2020[5]). In one interview, it was mentioned that these changes in personnel imply many times that the public manager who receives the audit observations is not the same manager who was audited. The often large time gap between the audit and the issuing of the audit report already mentioned above exacerbates this issue.

This comes along with two challenges. On the one hand, the new managers may not feel concerned and feel no ownership of the observations in the report. They feel that the observation is addressed to the previous responsible official and thus provides a room to rationalise non-action by saying that this was not under their responsibility. On the other hand, more practically, this situation sometimes creates issues in the ability to address efficiently the observations, as the institutional memory has been lost with the manager that left the position and that it may be difficult and time consuming to obtain the information that may date back several years. Beyond staff rotation, this issue is also related to weaknesses of internal information management and the archives of the services.

Third, as mentioned above, the interaction of public managers with the audit teams from the CGR is usually quite limited. Internal audit staff as well reflected during interviews that they may not engage public managers enough and in a pro-active way. As such, CGR audits may simply not be salient for public managers and compete with other priorities and challenges in their day-to-day work.

References

Dirección de Presupuestos (2020), *Anuario Estadístico del Empleo Público en el Gobierno Central 2011-2019*. [5]

OECD (2021), *Preventive and Concomitant Control at Colombia's Supreme Audit Institution: New Strategies for Modern Challenges*, OECD Public Governance Reviews, OECD Publishing, Paris, https://doi.org/10.1787/a2bdadf3-en. [3]

OECD (2020), *Working Party of Senior Budget Officials Chile: Review of DIPRES Programme Evaluation System JT03460195 OFDE*, OECD, Paris. [1]

OECD (2016), *Progress in Chile's Supreme Audit Institution: Reforms, Outreach and Impact*, OECD Public Governance Reviews, OECD Publishing, Paris, https://doi.org/10.1787/9789264250635-en. [4]

OECD (2014), *Chile's Supreme Audit Institution: Enhancing Strategic Agility and Public Trust*, OECD Public Governance Reviews, OECD Publishing, Paris, https://doi.org/10.1787/9789264207561-en. [2]

3 Behaviourally-informed strategies to strengthen the uptake of audit reports in Chile

Insights from behavioural sciences can inspire several measures to increase the likelihood of the uptake of the audit reports issued by the CGR by the auditees. This chapter provides concrete recommendations to the Chilean SAI on measures that could be included during the auditing phase, measures that could enhance the audit reports and measures to motivate or build peer or social pressure during the follow-up process. A strategic perspective that combines several measures is most likely to generate impact and to contribute significantly to enhancing the relevance of CGR's audits.

Introduction

The analysis carried out showed that behavioural biases and barriers are relevant to understand why public officials in the audited services in Chile may fail to address audit observations issued by the Comptroller General of the Republic (*Contraloría General de la República*, CGR). Figure 3.1 provides a summary of the relevant behavioural aspects presented and discussed in Chapter 2. The behavioural insights lens applied throughout the auditing process could contribute significantly to improve the uptake of audit reports and therefore the impact of the CGR.

Figure 3.1. Summary of main challenges to the uptake of audit reports in Chile

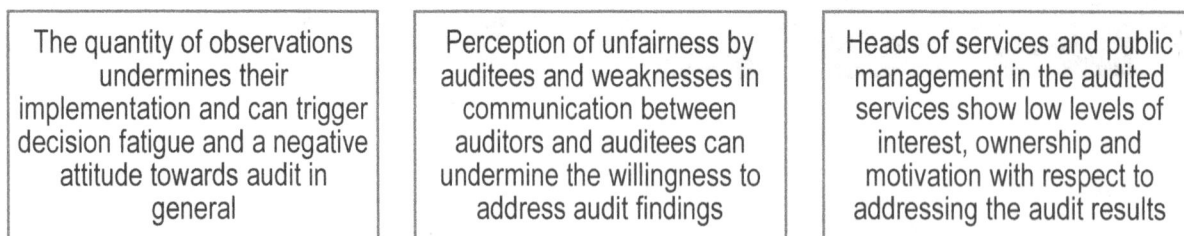

The quantity of observations undermines their implementation and can trigger decision fatigue and a negative attitude towards audit in general	Perception of unfairness by auditees and weaknesses in communication between auditors and auditees can undermine the willingness to address audit findings	Heads of services and public management in the audited services show low levels of interest, ownership and motivation with respect to addressing the audit results

In fact, as mentioned previously, considering behavioural dimensions in auditing processes is not new (Kida, 1984[1]; Kinney and Uecker, 1982[2]; Kassin, Dror and Kukucka, 2013[3]). Various guidelines and standards refer more or less explicitly to behavioural dimensions. For instance, Box 3.1 displays good practices that can influence the impact of SAIs reported by EUROSAI; they contain several relevant recommendations that can inspire interventions to promote behavioural change. INTOSAI also provides guidance for SAIs on improving the use and impact of audit reports and emphasises the following aspects that are all relevant from a behavioural perspective (INTOSAI, 2010[4]):

- *Salience:* When selecting audits, make sure that topics are useful and consult stakeholders before starting an audit;
- *Quality assurance and clarity:* Building in quality throughout the audit process in line with ISSAI standards, and ensuring that auditees know what to expect. Audit reports should be written using plain language and short sentence structures and include an executive summary to highlight main findings;
- *Communication:* Communicate results of audits clearly and effectively and invite auditees and stakeholders to give feedback on audit reports;
- *Follow-up:* Find out if progress has been made through systematic tracking and monitoring of uptake of recommendations, and where necessary, initiating follow-up audits when no progress has been made.

Box 3.1. Good practices and corresponding factors that influence SAI's impact

In the context of improving the implementation of audit recommendations to achieve impact, a recent EUROSAI report defines a good practice as a procedure (legal or other), method or other practice that can contribute to the appropriate and timely implementation of audit recommendations issued by the SAI. As such, EUROSAI reformulates the influencing factors on impact as a chronological listing of good practices throughout the audit process (Table 3.1).

Table 3.1. Good practices and corresponding factors that influence impact

Factors that influence the impact of SAIs	Good practice
Audit report quality	• Write relevant, operational and targeted recommendations. • Classify the recommendations in order of importance.
Constructive relationship between auditor and auditee	• Seek acceptance of the recommendations by the auditee, thereby increasing the support base. • Engage the auditee or the government in the follow-up of the implementation of recommendations. • Ask the auditee for an action plan that specifies the measures to implement the recommendations, including deadlines. • Check the appropriateness of the action plan. • In the absence of an action plan, set clear and realistic deadlines for the implementation of the recommendations, if possible in agreement with the auditee.
Existence of follow-up system	• Set clear and realistic deadlines for the implementation of recommendations. • Provide for an effective recommendation monitoring and follow-up system that checks the implementation in a timely manner. • Repeat this follow-up, or even consider a follow-up audit, in case there is no adequate implementation or insufficient information about the implementation.
Parliamentary involvement	• Engage parliament in the follow-up of the implementation of recommendations.
Use of the follow-up results for the performance monitoring system and the risk assessment	• Use the results of the follow-up system for risk assessment or a performance monitoring system.

Source: (EUROSAI, 2021[5]).

To clarify where the CGR could introduce behaviourally inspired measures, Figure 3.2 simplifies the follow-up process described in Chapter 2. The Figure shows the actors whose behaviours could be targeted to generate the desired impact and underscores the value added of looking at the whole process from a behavioural perspective.

Figure 3.2. Entry points for potential behavioural interventions to improve audit uptake in Chile

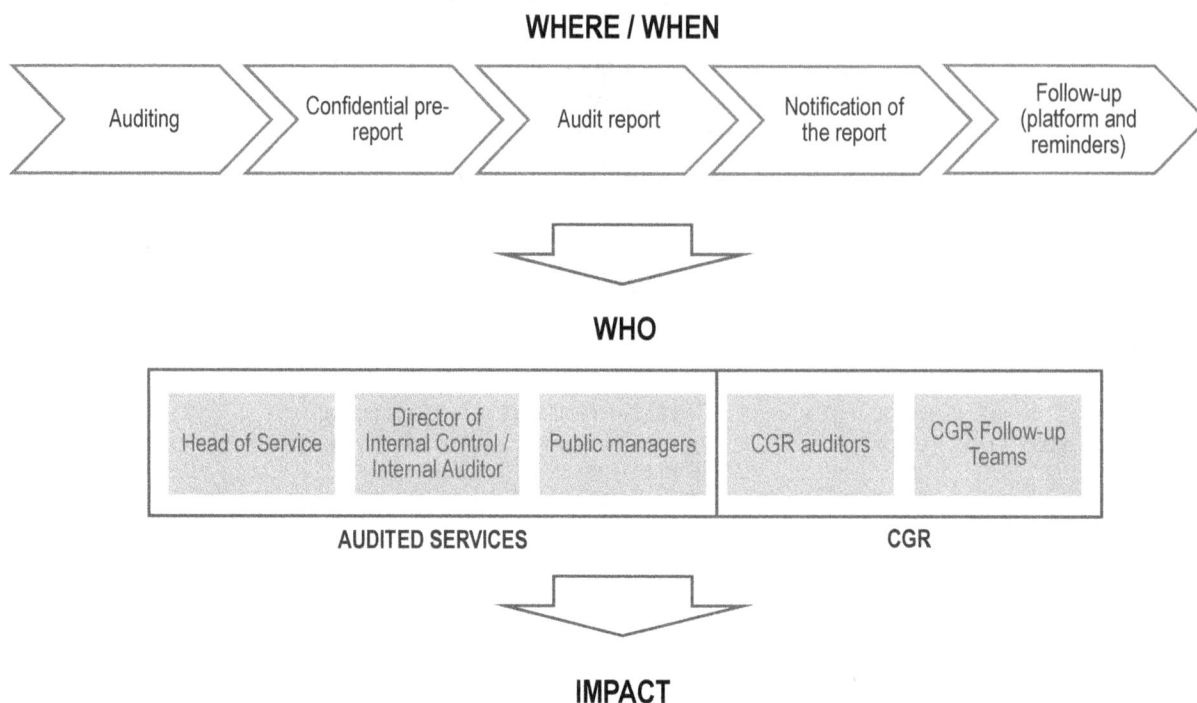

WHERE / WHEN

| Auditing | Confidential pre-report | Audit report | Notification of the report | Follow-up (platform and reminders) |

WHO

| Head of Service | Director of Internal Control / Internal Auditor | Public managers | CGR auditors | CGR Follow-up Teams |

AUDITED SERVICES — CGR

IMPACT

Narrow behavioural interventions aimed at nudging a behaviour of one of the actors in a specific step of the audit process as depicted in Figure 3.2 may succeed in changing this target behaviour, but may fail at generating an impact at the level of the uptake of audit recommendations. This impact typically depends on several behaviours of various actors.

Figure 3.3 provides a simplified overview on the underlying rationale. Suppose that there are several relevant behaviours (B) throughout an audit process that are relevant for explaining its impact. A behavioural analysis may have identified one behaviour, e.g. B_5, and achieved to change this behaviour, for example through a nudge. However, this change alone may not be sufficient to impact on the overall objective to improve the uptake of the audit if the other behaviours, or at least several of them, are not addressed as well. Therefore, impact is likely to be stronger and more sustainable if the CGR implements several adjustments throughout its audit processes.

Figure 3.3. To generate impact, behavioural changes at different levels may typically be required

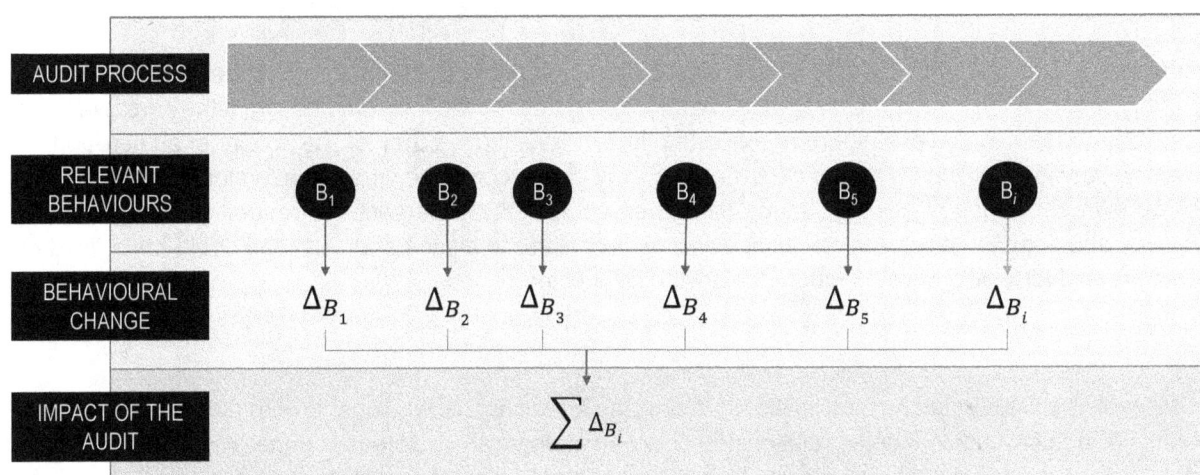

This idea of implementing complementary measures aiming at changes at different steps of the audit process, as also emphasised by EUROSAI in the Box above (EUROSAI, 2021[5]), is reflected in the following sections. The analysis identified six behaviourally inspired strategies that could help promoting change leading ultimately to impact in the uptake of CGR's audit reports. According to the priorities, resources and opportunities, the CGR could consider combining several selected measures proposed in these strategies.

The six strategies, that will be presented in the following sections, are:

- Implement measures to improve the auditor-auditee relationship throughout an audit cycle by increasing interactions and making these more constructive.

- Promote a cultural change within the CGR towards more supportive attitudes towards auditees by building relevant internal capacities, by targeting supervisors and leaders and by making good practices visible.

- Review the drafting of the audit reports to make them more user-friendly by simplifying them and by providing more guidance.

- Improve the response of auditees by testing different messages to notify about the audit report.

- Target frustration and promote better quality responses by allowing for a better planning, by introducing some flexibility with the deadlines and by tracking advances.

- Creating public or peer pressure through a reporting of the follow-up results.

Achieving impact through measures targeting auditors of the CGR

As emphasised in Chapter 2, the behaviour of CGR auditors while conducting an audit can affect the behaviour of the auditees with respect to the implementation of the audit observations. In fact, as mentioned previously, unconscious biases of auditors can lead them to be overly critical and orient their search design towards evidence confirming their prior beliefs (Pennington, Schafer and Pinsker, 2017[6]).

In Chile, anecdotal evidence of fraud and corruption or mismanagement could indeed frame CGR auditors towards a negative attitude that is likely to affect both the quantity of observations and a constructive and open attitude on the receiver side, thereby reducing the likelihood of taking corrective actions. As described above, social norms in the CGR can exacerbate this vicious cycle. The following measures therefore aim to improve the auditor-auditee relationship by more and more constructive interactions and by promoting a cultural change within the CGR towards a more supportive attitude.

Implement measures to improve the auditor-auditee relationship throughout an audit cycle by increasing interactions and making these more constructive

Interviews evidenced that interactions between auditors and public managers are scarce and usually quite formal. Currently, the involvement of public managers is limited to the kick-off meeting, if they are available, and when presenting the pre-report. At the same time, it was flagged that for the uptake of audit reports, it would be key to involve public managers more actively to overcome the inherent aversion against change, seeing own errors and prevent pro forma disagreement with the observations. In addition, the qualitative analysis showed that at least some audit observations relate to issues that auditees could have fixed on site if the auditor would have communicated with the auditee.

Potential measures

In general, the CGR could gain by investing in building a continuous relationship with auditees beyond the context of specific audits. A better relationship between auditors and auditees in general is likely to promote positive reciprocity between the actors. In the Netherlands, regular meetings between the SAI and the assembled heads of internal audit allow to discuss audit plans and risk analysis, for example. Belgium's SAI conducts informal meetings at the beginning and the end of the audit process.

Chile therefore could consider establishing similar practices to generate better interactions between auditors and auditees before, during and after the on-site audit process.

- **Improve interaction *before* the audit.** Engaging auditees before the audit to explain its rationale is likely to increase both the willingness to co-operate and the motivation of auditees. The CGR could review the dynamics of the current kick-off meeting to allow for a more constructive approach and to address potential feelings of being treated unfairly. The kick-off meeting provides the opportunity to explain the underlying standards and the rationale for the audit as well as to clarify the audit criteria and the risk-based methodology used to determine the CGR's annual audit planning (Box 3.2). Auditees that have the feeling of being audited too often could see the strategic value of the upcoming audit as an opportunity to reverse this trend and to reduce their level of risk by addressing the audit observations. A positive setting during the meeting could contribute to striking the delicate balance between maintaining independence and building mutual empathy.

Box 3.2. Informing the auditee what to expect during the executions of an audit

Auditees can be involved during the execution of an audit by setting up communication protocols between the SAI and the auditee that identify the following:

- The responsibilities of the SAI and the auditee
- Guidance on key stages of the audit process
- Which documents will be shared between the SAI and auditee
- How the SAI will let the auditee know about upcoming audits
- Information about the audit plan, timeframe, audit methodology
- Type of information and access to be provided by auditee
- How and when emerging findings will be shared
- When the auditee will receive a copy of the draft report

Source: https://www.idi.no/elibrary/well-governed-sais/sais-engaging-with-stakeholders/697-idi-sais-engaging-with-stakeholders-guide/file.

- **Increase interaction *during* the on-site audit process:** The potential behavioural impact of increasing reciprocity between the actors could be maximised by introducing feedback and interaction steps all along the audit process ("tit for tat" logic). For instance, engaging auditees at the beginning will be more efficient if auditees know they can reciprocate later in the process during follow-up meetings. For instance, the CGR could develop a protocol for auditors providing guidance on how to create more spaces of interactions with auditees in the field before drafting the report. Auditors could present preliminary results of the audit to managers for their feedback and thereby build a constructive relationship. The CGR already has internal good practices on which to build on (Box 3.3) and are currently considering to require as a minimum two meetings between auditors and auditees during an audit. In addition, the CGR has already instructed auditors to allow auditees to correct directly, if possible, minor observations. This approach could be further supported by providing guidance to the auditors on how to provide ad hoc support to the auditees in the field. Making such advocacy behaviour by auditors more salient within the CGR and perhaps establishing incentives for it, also contributes to changing the culture of "the more observations the better" and to take a more supportive attitude towards auditees (see the following section).

Box 3.3. Auditing the SDG's in Chile: Good practice to communicate with auditees

The CGR in Chile recognises the value of an improved communication during the audit process to achieve improvements in the processes of the audited services, which should be the ultimate objective of any audit.

While audits of national entities provide a single opportunity for feedback by auditees during the pre-report stage, the team of United Nations auditors of the CGR follows a different methodology. Prior to the publication of the final audit report, several memos (Audit Observation Memorandum, AOM) are delivered to the auditees informing them of the preliminary observations, which allows them to respond and clarify what observed. Later, all AOM are consolidated in a document called Management Letter, which reflects the findings, the respective analysis of the auditees' response to the AOM, the conclusion of the audit team to the observed facts, the recommendations and the client's position regarding these recommendations, indicating whether the auditee accepts or rejects the recommendations suggested. The document includes an annex with the status of implementation of the pending recommendations.

Source: Information provided by the CGR Chile.

- **Improve interaction *after* the on-site audit process.** The CGR could discuss preliminary findings with auditees during an exit meeting. The discussion could focus on clarifying doubts and on getting feedback concerning the feasibility of corrective actions from the auditees. For the design of such meetings, the experiences from Brazil and Belgium could be particularly interesting (Box 3.4).
  - The exit meeting could take place before issuing the final report. Changes agreed upon during this exit meeting could be included in the final audit report. Being able to influence the final report is likely to have a positive effect on the ownership of the report by the auditees. A recent EUROSAI report finds that some SAIs in Europe ask the auditees explicitly to indicate whether they agree, partly agree or disagree with each recommendation. Those SAI then have to review rejected recommendations on a higher administrative level. Some SAIs with a jurisdictional model, mainly in the area of compliance audits, even negotiate the recommendations with the auditee to avoid non-feasible or non-realistic recommendations. In case of a non-agreement, auditees can formulate a complaint against the audit report (EUROSAI, 2021[5]).

- o Alternatively, and more relevant in the Chilean context, the CGR could consider a meeting between CGR and the audited service after issuing the final audit report but before starting the follow-up process. The objective of the meeting would be to explain the observations, clarify doubts and to recommend certain lines of actions the management could take to address them. Chapter 4 provides a more detailed theory of change for this measure and guidance for the implementation of a potential pilot.

Box 3.4. Post-audit exit meetings in Brazil and Belgium

The Office of the Comptroller General of the Union (*Controladoria-Geral da União*, CGU), responsible for internal audits in Brazil, carries out a meeting with auditees to discuss the findings and together find potential solutions ("*reunião de busca conjunta de soluções*"). The CGU auditors present the findings and decide together with the auditees if these observations can be addressed directly, and, if that is the case, the observations can be eliminated from the audit report.

In Belgium, the SAI (*Rekenhof*) has established informal exit meetings after the audit process and before writing the report, where the auditor presents the recommendations that will be included in the report. According to information provided by the Belgian SAI, these informal exit meetings seem to improve the acceptance of the reports by the auditees.

Source: OECD, based on information provided by the CGU and the Belgian Rekenhof.

Promote a cultural change within the CGR towards more supportive attitudes towards auditees

As described in Chapter 2, social norms shaping the organisational culture of the CGR affect the interactions between auditors and auditees. The informal norm according to which a good auditor produces many findings and observations still seems to dominate within the CGR and influences the behaviours of auditors. This norm also undermines the idea of allowing auditees to address some issues directly on the spot, as these then will not be reflected in the audit report anymore. More generally, the norm tends to favour a critical and negative view with respect to auditees. It primes auditors that behave "severely" with auditees leading, again, to more observations and/or to maintain observations despite good arguments brought forward by the auditees.

Shifting social norms to impact on organisational cultures is complex, takes time and is an incremental process. To achieve change, the application of behavioural insights to organisations consists in influencing specific individuals in those organisations to affect organisation-wide changes or in directly intervening on organisational routines, policies, and procedures of the organisation, as emphasised in recent work of the OECD on safety culture in organisations (OECD, 2020[7]). This work also provides an overview on some key theoretical foundations and insights from organisational psychology when it comes to influencing organisational behaviour (Box 3.5).

Box 3.5. Applying Behavioural Insights to Organisations: Theoretical Foundations

When enough people are nudged toward behavioural change, those new behaviours have the potential to become habit, switching from deliberate choices and actions otherwise known as controlled processing, to less deliberate, less effortful, more habitual actions known as automatic processing. Whether deliberate or effortful, choice or habit, when enough people in a work group or entire organisation behave in a certain way, that behaviour has the potential to become a norm. Norms are rules for expected and accepted behaviour. As humans, violating norms tends to make us uncomfortable. We are likely to conform to the norms of our work group and organisation. This is especially true of cohesive groups who feel a degree of attraction to their work group.

Nudging supervisors or other powerful or influential people within an organisation can have a multiplying effect such that the behaviours exhibited and endorsed by influential individuals have a better chance of being adopted *en masse*, nudging a whole organisation in the process. Indeed, charismatic and transformational leaders are believed to possess qualities that inspire followers to behave in desired ways in service of a larger goal. Nudging such leaders can effect largescale behavioural change.

Of course, those in formal leadership roles toward the top of the organisational hierarchy are also in a good position to effect widespread behavioural change by altering organisational policies and procedures. Nudges that help high-level decision makers (leaders, boards, etc.) optimise organisational policy decisions in the face of their own biases and irrationalities can have an effect. Thus, helping decision makers see the connection between policies, procedures, and behaviour on the ground is another way to nudge whole organisations.

Source: (OECD, 2020[7]).

Potential measures

The CGR could consider implementing measures aimed at building capacities for strengthening a constructive audit approach and work towards transforming the organisational culture to promote a change in the behaviour of auditors. This could be achieved, for example, through the following measures.

- **Improve capacity building.** The CGR has an extensive internal policy for building capacities and promoting continuous learning. The trainings focus on technical auditing skills, such as legal aspects or accounting practices, and some are targeting "soft skills". To complement these efforts, the CGR could consider piloting a training for auditors aimed at building skills related to strengthening an "advocacy attitude", creating a constructive dialogue and preparing them to explain the rationale of an audit process to auditees in clear and friendly terms.

- **Promote cultural change.** To complement the training programmes, the CGR could aim at nudging a critical mass of officials in the CGR such that the new desired behaviour becomes a social norm in the institution (OECD, 2020[7]).

  - Knowing how others behave can be a powerful driver for own behaviour. For instance, in the United Kingdom, the Chief Medical Officer sent a letter to selected general practices notifying them that they were prescribing more antibiotics than 80% of the practices in their local area. As a result, 73 406 fewer prescriptions were made across 791 intervention practices, compared to the control group of 790 practices (Hallsworth et al., 2016[8]). Similarly, auditors could receive messages highlighting behaviours of other auditors that are more advocacy-focused.

  - Nudging leaders, those with formal or informal influence, is a way to nudge entire organisations (OECD, 2020[7]). The Comptroller General, together with the senior leadership of the CGR, could lead an internal awareness-raising campaign thematising and addressing the issue of the informal culture and its negative repercussions on generating impact while emphasising the potential of an organisational culture that supports change in the public administration.

    ○ Supervisors and heads of units in the middle management are setting an example by their own behaviour and by providing guidance to their teams and communicating to them (OECD, 2020[9]). Middle management could be sensitised to the behavioural challenges faced by auditees and trained to transmit these messages to their teams during day-to-day practice, performance evaluations or, for example, in the context of a mentoring programme.

Achieving impact through measures targeting the drafting and communication of the audit reports

Audit reports are the main official vehicle to communicate the audit findings and recommendations. SAIs that focus on clarity and drawing crosscutting conclusions will help to focus the minds of public leaders and managers. For example, useful SAI tools could include sector-based reports, systematic use of executive summaries, tagging key words or providing findings in a systematic way that allows for text and data mining (OECD, 2016[10]). SAIs are already encouraged to make their audit reports accessible and concise (INTOSAI, 2010[11]) and use a more positive tone. For instance, the revised government auditing standards of the United States Government Accountability Office (GAO) state the following:

> *"The report may recognize the positive aspects of the program reviewed if applicable to the audit objectives. Inclusion of positive program aspects may lead to improved performance by other government organizations that read the report. Audit reports are more objective when they demonstrate that the work has been performed by professional, unbiased, independent, and knowledgeable personnel" (GAO, 2018[12]).*

Therefore, the CGR could review the way audit reports are drafted and promote a new internal standard that takes into account behavioural dimensions of the receivers. Communicating this new standard contributes to make it salient within the organisation. Currently, the CGR audit reports contain a lot of information and focus extensively on explaining the audit methodology. In fact, some interview partners suggested that there might be a culture amongst public managers of not reading the audit reports. Overall, the CGR could benefit from reviewing both the content and the communication of the audit reports with a view to generate the expected change in auditee's behaviour.

Review the drafting of the audit reports

The analysis showed that the language of the audit report as well as the quantity (and sometimes quality) of observations may trigger a negative attitude towards the audit results and delay taking corrective actions. Auditees reported feeling sometimes overwhelmed by the observations and stated that they do not receive enough guidance. The measures to improve the auditor-auditee relationship could address part of the problem by clarifying and reducing the quantity of observations during the audit phase.

In addition, shorter reports focused on the findings and providing recommendations for addressing the observations in a simpler and less technical-legal language could facilitate the understanding, increase the motivation to act and thereby improve the impact of the reports. For example, Ireland's report on applying behavioural science in the tax administration explores how compliance can be improved through better and simpler presentation of information and by drawing attention to key facts (Customs, 2017[13]). Ideally, auditors write their reports with the auditee in mind (Box 3.6).

Box 3.6. Writing audit reports with audience awareness

The content of audit reports should be organised by its importance to the audit client. To them, seeing and understanding the results is more important than knowing how the results were found. According to the authors, audit reports should not all follow the same template. Decisions about what to include, what to leave out, and how to organise the report should be made based on awareness of the audience. Writing with audience awareness will help auditors overcome the task-oriented mind-set that results in audit-focused reports (Table 3.2).

Table 3.2. Recommendations to writing audit reports with audience awareness

Activity	What this means for audit report writers
Analysing or constructing a hypothetical audience	Conceptualise the report's audience. Who are they? What are their roles? What are their needs? What are their goals? Likes/dislikes? How do they perceive me?
Setting goals and naming plans aimed at a specific audience	Identify the intended takeaway from the report. What do you want the audience to understand? What do you want them to do? What is most important?
Evaluating content and style (persona) with regard to anticipated audience response	Consider how the audience will respond to the content and style of the report. Is the style appropriate for the audience? Is the style appropriate for the audit subject matter? Does the style affect whether the information will be received in a desirable or undesirable way?
Reviewing, editing, and revising for a specific audience	Systematically review and improve the text, keeping the audience in mind. Does it speak the language of the audience? Does it achieve its communication goals based on perceptions of the audience?

Source: (Cassels, Alvero and Errington, 2009[14]), adapted from Carol Berkenkotter's "Understanding a Writer's Awareness of Audience," College Composition and Communication, Vol. 32, No. 4 (December 1981), 388–399.

Source: https://www.iia.nl/actualiteit/nieuws/shift-your-audit-focus-%E2%80%8Bits-not-about-you, (Cassels, Alvero and Errington, 2009[14])

Potential measures

The CGR could continue improving the drafting of audit reports to make them more impactful. For example, this could be achieved by:

- **Reducing the technical and legal language.** Plain language means avoiding jargon or obscure words whenever possible. It also means explaining any technical or legal terms that are used to make audit reports more readable, especially those reports that address complex subjects. Exhibits, including illustrations, tables, charts or text boxes can help to attract a stakeholder's attention and reinforce key points (OECD, 2014[15]). As such, the CGR could consider running an experiment testing a sample of auditee's responses to hypothetical language changes using, for example, an experimental vignette methodology (EVM) (Aguinis and Bradley, 2014[16]; Atzmüller and Steiner, 2010[17]).

- **Reducing the size of the audit report.** Shorter reports are easier to read and could improve their relevance for the auditees, while potentially also reducing the time and costs involved in preparing the audit reports. Shorter reports focus on results and not on describing the details of the audit process. For example, legal and technical details could be provided as an annex to the main report. In addition, while all audit reports currently include executive summaries, the CGR could consider focusing the messages included in these summaries to outline the strategic value and objectives of the audit report in plain language.

- **Reducing, where possible, the quantity of observations in the reports.** Reports could, for example, group observations by project or process or emphasise underlying issues of which the observations are merely the symptoms. While the number of observations would remain the same, the logical packaging in bundles could make the report easier to digest and to see the strategic value. In addition, auditors could draw general conclusions with respect to the underlying weaknesses in the audited entities to explain the audit findings and hence the observations. As one CGR auditor stated: "*We should diagnose the sickness and not just describe the symptoms.*"

- **Include recommendations for corrective actions.** The CGR recently began to promote the inclusion of recommendations for corrective actions. This is a step towards providing clearer guidance to auditees, while paying caution no to co-administrate. The CGR could thus further promote the drafting of observations that are more action-oriented, e.g. by providing trainings to auditors. In addition, auditors should aim at emphasising the rationale underlying the observations to make it easier for public managers to understand their relevance and why they should care. Finally, observations and proposals for corrective actions should be drafted using plain, simple and straightforward language to become SMART recommendations (Box 3.7).

Box 3.7. Drafting SMART audit recommendations

Audit recommendations should be specific, measurable, achievable, realistic and timely (SMART):

- **S**: Specific recommendations correctly identify who is responsible for taking clear, corrective action to eliminate a deficiency and improve a public programme or activity.

- **M**: Measurable recommendations can be tracked by the SAI's follow-up system. SAIs can determine whether corrective actions were taken and deficiencies were eliminated. When implemented, recommendations should prevent recurrence of findings and allow the SAI to conduct an independent audit of the new conditions in the public programme.

- **A**: Achievable recommendations are doable in a reasonable period of time with available financial resources.

- **R**: Realistic recommendations recognise the priorities and operating constraints of the officials who are responsible for implementing them.

- **T**: Timely recommendations are provided to responsible officials at the right moment and manner to facilitate their prompt implementation.

Source: OECD.

Testing different messages to notify about the audit report

The findings showed that there may be negative predisposition, frustration or lack of interest by different actors in the audited service. In addition to improving interactions between auditors and auditees during an audit and the drafting of the audit reports, the CGR could consider framing the messages contained in the formal communications by the CGR.

Indeed, evidence from several behavioural insights applications around the world indicate that the way messages are framed can affect significantly the responses of the recipients (OECD, 2017[18]). For instance, an intervention carried out by the United Kingdom's Financial Conduct Authority (FCA) to promote compliance could inspire a similar intervention by the CGR targeted to audited services (see Box 3.8 below).

Potential measures

The CGR could consider an experiment to test which message generates the highest desired impact. For instance, the CGR could send different versions of the letters that are joined to the audit reports to a sample of services, stratified according to characteristics and then randomly selected to treatment and control groups to determine the messages that are most suited to promote compliance with observations.

Potential letters could be framed along the following messages:

- Highlight potential negative consequences for the Service.
- Highlight peer / social pressure ("X% of the services already complied with ...").
- Highlight positive associations such as trust, pride or commitment.
- Highlight the individual responsibility of the head of the service and/or Director of Internal Control.

Box 3.8. Improving submissions to the Financial Conduct Authority by mutual societies

United Kingdom's Financial Conduct Authority (FCA) tested specific messages when communicating with societies, which would draw their attention and encourage them to submit their annual return and accounts on time. Between 2013 and 2014, the FCA sent letters to a sample of 7 984 societies who were stratified by type of organisation, the month of their financial year-end and the last year they took action, and then randomly allocated to different treatments or to a control group. The treatments were:

- **Bullets**: Including salient bullet points and a message about penalties: "Last year mutual societies like yours were fined up to GBP 3 000 for failing to provide this information on time"
- **Warning**: Adding a warning to the envelope: "It is a legal obligation to complete and return the enclosed form", and
- **Timing**: Sending the letters on different dates (26 May, 3 June or 8 July). This helped the FCA to estimate the effects of the length of time between the letter and the deadline on compliance.

Of the societies in the trial, 6 456 took action (80.9%), while 1 528 (19.1%) did not take any action. Examining each treatment, the FCA found that the bullets and warning treatments failed to change the behaviour of societies compared to the control. However, the timing of the letters did affect the firms' response. Societies who received a letter in July (and who therefore had, on average, a shorter deadline – median of 23 days for July rather than 66 for May and 58 for June) were 2.4 percentage points more likely to respond to the communication. Across all groups, those with a shorter deadline were more likely to respond than those with a longer deadline.

Source: (OECD, 2017[18]).

Achieving impact through measures during the follow-up process

Target frustration and promote better quality responses by allowing for a better planning, by introducing some flexibility with the deadlines and by tracking advances

The findings showed that deadlines may cause stress and frustrations and sometimes can be unrealistic or not adapted to the reality of the public administration. Currently, the deadlines to take corrective actions are limited and standard (15, 30 or 60 working days). In some cases, however, deadlines are not sufficient to introduce changes in institutional processes. This, added to the fact that many times the follow-up is carried out long after the deadline has expired, generates a feeling of unfairness as the services consider that they would have had more time to deliver a better response. In addition, interviews with public managers evidenced that managers would appreciate an opportunity to report partial progress made in addressing observations or in improving processes that may lead to prevent future observations.

EUROSAI emphasises that "defining deadlines in agreement with the auditee contributes to a good relationship and generates support for the implementation of the recommendations" (EUROSAI, 2021[5]). In the survey conducted by EUROSAI, out of 19 SAIs who set deadlines, nine determine the deadlines in agreement with the auditee, three let the auditees set their deadlines. Deadlines are fixed independently by six SAIs. This mostly applies to SAIs with legally binding recommendations.

Potential measures

In line with the previous recommendations, the CGR could promote a sense of support rather than strict control of the audited service by transmitting the idea that what really matters is improving public management and processes in the audited entities, not the fact of complying with deadlines.

As such, to reduce stress of non-compliance and motivate public managers, the CGR could consider the following measures:

- When discussing the pre-report or when discussing the follow-up process, the CGR could allow for some flexibility concerning the deadlines for addressing the observations case-by-case, involving the Internal Auditors or the Directors of Internal Control and the public managers responsible for the processes with observations. The decision to adapt deadlines would need to respond to clear and homogenous pre-established criteria to ensure fairness and could show flexibility and improve the willingness of public managers to take action, as they will be personally committed to the deadline. Chapter 4 provides more details on this measure in view of carrying out a potential pilot.

- During the interviews, auditees proposed to create a mechanism through which services can report partial progress or planned actions to address observations. Such a mechanism could also provide an opportunity to report difficulties inherent to the nature of the process related to the observation. For instance, the CGR could consider including intermediate corrective actions with specific deadlines. In this way, auditees could communicate progress made in resolving an observation.

- Sometimes, public managers do not meet deadlines because of the workload or because they simply forgot about it. As described in Chapter 2, the CGR online follow-up system automatically generates reminders before deadlines are due. Nonetheless, the CGR could test different reminders created by the online follow-up system in view of finding the most effective nudges to take actions.

- According to the interviews, the stress related to the deadlines results sometimes from the fact that auditees do not know when exactly to expect the audit report. This makes it difficult for them to plan. Therefore, the CGR could consider notifying the services well in advance of sending the audit pre-report. The OECD already recommended that the CGR could provide information on when the audited entity could expect to receive the preliminary audit report for comments at the beginning of the audit process (OECD, 2014[15]). The CGR could review its internal drafting and review process to identify a step in this internal process that could allow sending, well in advance, a message communicating at least a likely timeframe of when the pre-report will be sent to the service.

Creating public or peer pressure through a reporting of the follow-up results

Arguably, the performance of audited services in addressing observations indicate their willingness to improve and to comply with regulations and procedures. As mentioned previously and evidenced in Figure 1.4 in Chapter 1, 65.2% of SAI's in OECD countries with available data publicly report on actions taken by the executive to address audit recommendations. In Latin America, only 25% of countries do so. Chile is not amongst these countries. Indeed, research has shown that providing public information on audit reports can significantly reduce the probability of re-electing a mayor in which at least two violations associated with corruption were reported (Ferraz and Finan, 2008[19]; Avis, Ferraz and Finan, 2018[20]). A recent EUROSAI report based on a survey also emphasises that reporting the follow-up results to a broader audience can raise the pressure on the auditees in case of insufficient implementation or provide positive incentives to well-performing auditees (EUROSAI, 2021[5]). Out of 33 respondents, 20 SAI in Europe do publish a global report on the follow-up of audit reports (Figure 3.4). Finally, INTOSAI recommends that the results of SAIs' follow-up exercises should be communicated publicly, unless regulations stipulate otherwise (INTOSAI, 2010[4]).

Figure 3.4. In Europe, the majority of SAIs issue reports on follow-up of audit reports

Does your SAI make a global report on the follow-up of recommendations/reports and is it communicated to external stakeholders?

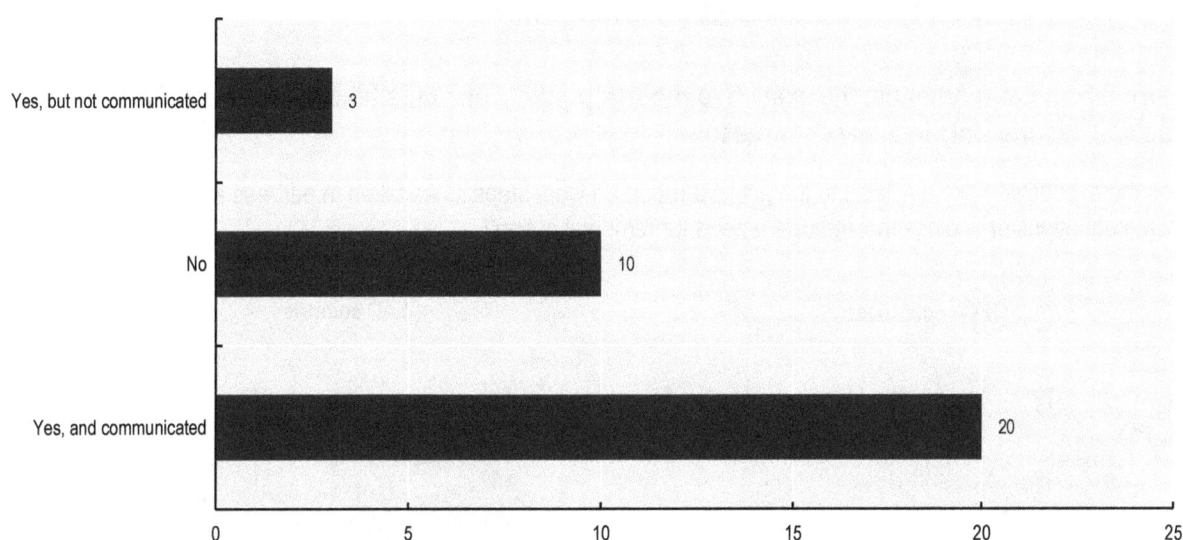

Note: 33 respondents.
Source: (EUROSAI, 2021[5]).

Potential measures

In Chile, interviews emphasised that the heads of services typically have only very limited interest and incentive to internally follow-up on audit reports and ensure the implementation of corrective actions. Therefore, to provide stronger incentives, the CGR could consider making non-compliance with audit reports more salient to heads of services and/or make this information visible to the public to facilitate accountability.

- The CGR could test the impact of adding information to the letters sent with the audit reports on how the service has performed in taking corrective actions over the past years. This information could be non-public, directed only to the highest authority of the service. Some Offices of Inspector General (OIG) in the US provide management reports signed by the head of the OIG and sent to the head of the agency, which are tracking open issues and are holding leadership accountable.

- The CGR could make non-compliance more visible to the public. To do so, the CGR could build on their good practices in transparency and in communicating with citizens (OECD, 2014[15]; OECD, 2016[21]). At municipal level, for example, the reports of the CGR may trigger social accountability processes asking for the reasons of non-compliance. In turn, including recognition of services with better behaviour or providing information to the public regarding services that perform better in addressing observations could have a political value for heads of services and set incentives to introducing improvements to their institutional processes.

- The CGR could explore possibilities to promote some kind of benchmarking to promote yardstick competition between services. However, due care must be taken to ensure that the services are compared with other services that are truly similar, for instance in terms of size, level of risks and budget, to avoid any negative impact on the perceived fairness of such a comparison. This is particularly important taking into account the quantitative analyses in Chapter 2 showing a high concentration of observations in a few entities. Therefore, such a benchmarking could be relevant for the municipal level in particular, as municipalities are comparable in terms of the public services they provide and could be clustered by size and budget, for example.

- Finally, while most countries in LAC and the majority of OECD countries do not require the executive to publicly report on the measures taken to address the audit recommendations (Figure 3.5), Chile could consider requiring services to report publicly on the steps they have taken to address all, most or some findings in the audit reports.

Figure 3.5. In Latin America, the executive reports *publicly* on steps taken to address findings from SAI audit reports only in a few countries

Does the executive make available to the public a report on what steps it has taken to address audit recommendations or findings that indicate a need for remedial action?

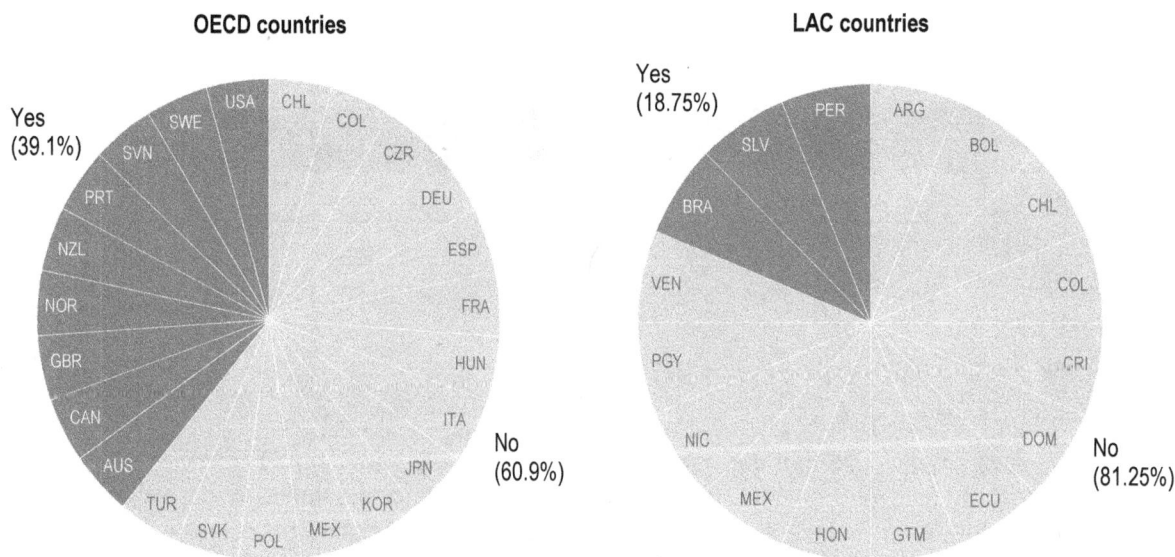

Note: The answer "yes" means that the executive reports publicly on (all, most or some) audit findings, while the answer "no" means that the executive does not report on steps it has taken to address audit findings.
Source: International Budget Partnership, Open Budget Survey 2019.

References

Aguinis, H. and K. Bradley (2014), "Best Practice Recommendations for Designing and Implementing Experimental Vignette Methodology Studies", *Organizational Research Methods*, Vol. 17/4, pp. 351-371, https://doi.org/10.1177/1094428114547952. [16]

Atzmüller, C. and P. Steiner (2010), "Experimental vignette studies n survey research", *Methodology*, Vol. 6/3, pp. 128-138, https://doi.org/10.1027/1614-2241/a000014. [17]

Avis, E., C. Ferraz and F. Finan (2018), "Do government audits reduce corruption? Estimating the impacts of exposing corrupt politicians", *Journal of Political Economy*, Vol. 126/5, pp. 1912-1964, https://doi.org/10.1086/699209. [20]

Cassels, W., K. Alvero and C. Errington (2009), *Internal auditors need to shift the focus of audit reporting from their own priorities to those of the client*, https://www.iia.nl/SiteFiles/IA/ia201904-dl_Itsnotaboutyou.pdf (accessed on 10 May 2021). [14]

Customs, I. (2017), *Applying Behavioural Science in Tax Administration - A Summary of Lessons Learned*. [13]

EUROSAI (2021), *Follow-up of the implementation of audit recommendations: Best practices guide, issued by the project group*, European Organisation of Supreme Audit Institutions (EUROSAI). [5]

Ferraz, C. and F. Finan (2008), "Exposing corrupt politicians: The effects of Brazil's publicly released audits on electoral outcomes", *The Quarterly Journal of Economics* May, pp. 703-745, http://papers.ssrn.com/sol3/papers.cfm?abstract_id=997867 (accessed on 30 December 2014). [19]

GAO (2018), *Government Auditing Standards 2018 Revision*, United States Government Accountability Office, http://www.gao.gov/yellowbook. (accessed on 10 May 2021). [12]

Hallsworth, M. et al. (2016), "Provision of social norm feedback to high prescribers of antibiotics in general practice: a pragmatic national randomised controlled trial", *www.thelancet.com*, Vol. 387, p. 1743, https://doi.org/10.1016/S0140-6736(16)00215-4. [8]

INTOSAI (2010), *How to increase the use and impact of audit reports: A guide for Supreme Audit Institutions*, INTOSAI Capacity Building Committee, https://iniciativatpa.org/wp-content/uploads/2014/05/Increase-impact-of-audit-reports.pdf (accessed on 28 September 2020). [4]

INTOSAI (2010), *How to increase the use and impact of audit reports: A guide for Supreme Audit Institutions*. [11]

Kassin, S., I. Dror and J. Kukucka (2013), "The forensic confirmation bias: Problems, perspectives, and proposed solutions", *Journal of Applied Research in Memory and Cognition*, Vol. 2/1, pp. 42-52, https://doi.org/10.1016/j.jarmac.2013.01.001. [3]

Kida, T. (1984), *The Impact of Hypothesis-Testing Strategies on Auditors' Use of Judgment Data*. [1]

Kinney, W. and W. Uecker (1982), *Mitigating the Consequences of Anchoring in Auditor Judgments*, https://www.jstor.org/stable/246739. [2]

OECD (2020), *Behavioural Insights and Organisations: Fostering Safety Culture*, OECD Publishing, Paris, https://doi.org/10.1787/e6ef217d-en. [7]

OECD (2020), *OECD Public Integrity Handbook*, OECD Publishing, Paris, https://doi.org/10.1787/ac8ed8e8-en. [9]

OECD (2017), *Behavioural Insights and Public Policy: Lessons from Around the World*, OECD Publishing, Paris, https://doi.org/10.1787/9789264270480-en. [18]

OECD (2016), *Progress in Chile's Supreme Audit Institution: Reforms, Outreach and Impact*, OECD Public Governance Reviews, OECD Publishing, Paris, https://doi.org/10.1787/9789264250635-en. [21]

OECD (2016), *Supreme Audit Institutions and Good Governance: Oversight, Insight and Foresight*, OECD Public Governance Reviews, OECD Publishing, Paris, https://doi.org/10.1787/9789264263871-en. [10]

OECD (2014), *Chile's Supreme Audit Institution: Enhancing Strategic Agility and Public Trust*, OECD Public Governance Reviews, OECD Publishing, Paris, https://doi.org/10.1787/9789264207561-en. [15]

Pennington, R., J. Schafer and R. Pinsker (2017), "Do Auditor Advocacy Attitudes Impede Audit Objectivity?", *Journal of Accounting, Auditing & Finance*, Vol. 32/1, pp. 136-151, https://doi.org/10.1177/0148558X16641862. [6]

4 Piloting a meeting to explain audit findings and the effects of more flexible deadlines in Chile

This chapter presents a detailed theory of change for two interventions taken from the strategies proposed in Chapter 3 and that could be piloted by the CGR. First, a meeting between the CGR and the audited services before starting the follow-up process could help explaining the audit findings, reduce the cognitive burden and provide avenues for taking corrective actions. Second, the CGR could introduce some flexibility with deadlines to signal credibly a supportive approach by the CGR. In addition, the chapter provides guidance on how to implement the pilot and measure results.

Selected pilot interventions

Achieving a sustainable positive impact on the uptake of audit reports is complex, is likely to require several reforms at different levels of the auditing and follow-up process and may require working towards a cultural change in both the Comptroller General of the Republic (*Contraloría General de la República*, CGR) and the administration. Therefore, in Chapter 3, the OECD recommends several measures that can be combined to achieve change and impact.

Together, the CGR and the OECD identified two measures that could be piloted to test their impact and learn during the implementation process before potentially scaling up the measures. Both interventions take place after the issuing of the audit report but before starting the follow-up process. They are complementary and aim at reducing auditees' cognitive burden and perceived stress and unfairness related to deadlines:

- **Measure A:** To support audited entities, the CGR could consider a meeting between CGR and the audited service before starting the follow-up process. The objective of the meeting is to explain the observations and to recommend certain lines of actions the management could take to address them, while paying caution not to co-administrate.

- **Measure B:** When discussing the follow-up process once the audit report has been finalised, the CGR could introduce some flexibility with the deadlines for addressing the observations on a case-by-case base, following clear and pre-established criteria, involving Internal Auditor or Directors of Internal Control and the public managers responsible for addressing the observations.

Both measures aim at facilitating the follow-up of the audit observations by auditees and at building a better relationship between auditors and auditees. The rationale for the choice of the two measures reflects the scope of the project, which focused on the follow-up process. It also addresses two main underlying causes that, according to the qualitative research undertaken and reported in Chapter 2, contribute to explain the level of uptake of audit reports in Chile. On the one hand, the attention bias and cognitive burden caused by too many observations and too complex audit reports and, on the other hand, the stress and the perception of auditees that the CGR does not understand or care about the realities of the public administration by imposing uniform deadlines. As such, Measure A is about content; Measure B is about the process. Notwithstanding, further criteria for the selection where *continuity*, as a similar idea as mentioned in Measure A has been discussed previously within the CGR, and *feasibility*, as both measures can be implemented and tested without requiring legal changes.

Theory of change

A theory of change identifies underlying assumptions about how change comes about, make these assumptions more explicit and test them (Johnsøn, 2012[1]; OECD, 2017[2]). Figure 4.1 below provides a schematic overview of the theory of change underlying the two measures. The mechanisms, two for each Measure, are the channels through which it is assumed that the Measures will contribute to results.

Figure 4.1. Theory of change of the pre-follow up meeting and the negotiation of deadlines

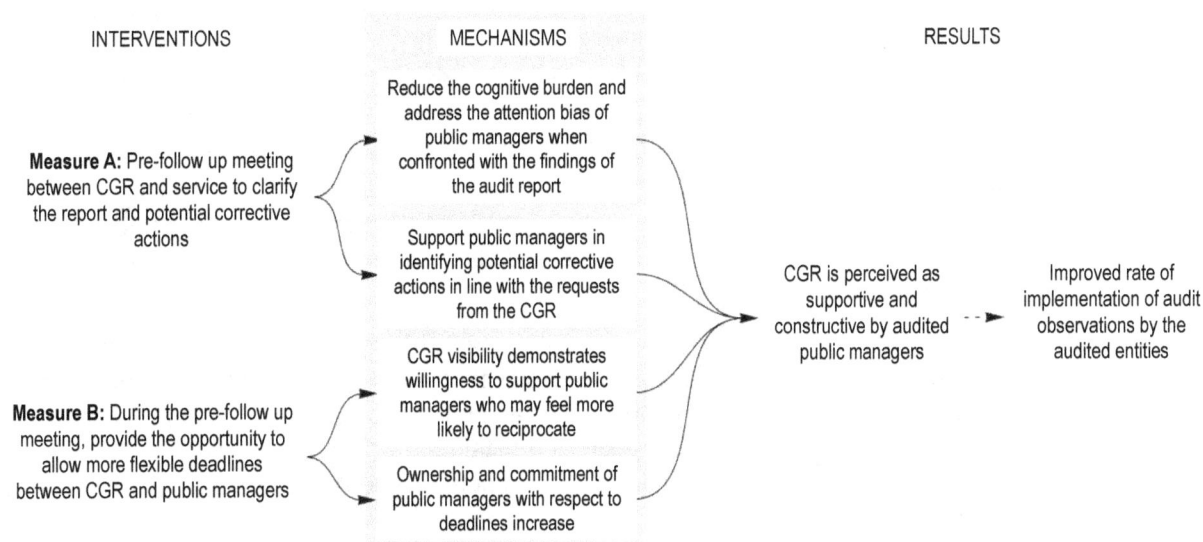

Measure A, the pre-follow up meeting between the CGR and the audited service, responds to a finding from Chapter 2 in so far that public managers expressed the desire to obtain better guidance on how to address concretely the observations and/or to have the opportunity to clarify these observations.

The theory of change behind the hypothesis that this meeting is likely to improve the uptake of the audit report relies on the following mechanisms (Figure 4.1):

- First, the meeting contributes to reducing the cognitive burden of public managers in the audited service when confronted with the final audit report. The meeting seeks to clarify and simplify the findings and observations in plain language and from the perspective of management. This, in turn, should impact on the relationship between auditors and auditees and lead to a more pro-active attitude and thus uptake of audit reports.

- Second, through the guidance provided by the CGR during the meeting with respect to potential avenues to take corrective actions, the likelihood that public managers will actually take action are likely to increase if the reason for inaction was related to a lack of knowledge concerning what to do. In addition, following the meeting, the probability of corrective actions that are not aligned with the expectations by the CGR, and thus remain as incomplete in the system, should be lower and therefore lead to higher rates of compliance. To avoid perceptions of co-administration and ensure ownership, these avenues for concrete corrective actions need to be elaborated by public managers, with support from the CGR.

Measure B is straightforward. Chapter 2 evidenced that public managers experience stress and frustration about the non-flexible and uniform deadlines imposed by the CGR. This has reportedly sometimes generated a feeling of being treated unfair or of being misunderstood ("*the CGR does not understand the realities of the public administration*"). Therefore, the possibility to have more flexibility with deadlines for taking corrective actions during the meeting proposed in Measure A, should allow addressing this issue.

The theory behind the hypothesis that negotiating the deadlines will improve the uptake of the audit report relies on the following mechanisms (Figure 4.1):

- First, by allowing deadlines that are more flexible on a case-by-case basis but following clear and pre-established criteria, the CGR visibly and credibly demonstrates flexibility and its willingness to support public managers. As human beings tend to reciprocate, this flexibility on the side of the CGR could increase public managers' motivation to comply with the audit reports.

- Second, having the public managers actively involved in fixing the deadlines could increase their sense of ownership. Public managers may feel personally committed to the deadline. In addition, it could be considered to reinforce this ownership and commitment by signing an informal pledge to comply with the deadline.

Overall, both the meeting and the possibility to negotiate deadlines could contribute to improve the relationship between the CGR and the audited services. As such, the design of the meeting should seek to promote a constructive environment, where the doubts and concerns of public managers are taken serious and where the CGR provides concrete support to facilitate the work of the public managers. The meeting should be communicated and implemented as support to public managers, not as another bureaucratic requirement.

Potentially, the meeting may have indirect effects on the way auditors will draft future reports, taking into account the feed-back they receive and the interactions they had during the meeting. For this, the CGR needs to ensure a feed-back loop from this meeting to auditors. The survey administered to auditors (see below) should take into account such a potential change in future behaviour.

Implementation design and measurement

Strictly speaking, impact can only be measured rigorously if the intervention takes into account the counterfactual, that is, what would have happened without the intervention (OECD, 2017[2]). For this, the universe needs to be big enough to allow for a sample size with sufficient statistical power and room to compare across intervention and control groups. However, given that the number of ongoing audits carried out by the CGR is likely to be insufficient to reach a sufficient sample size to implement such a randomised control trial methodology, the CGR could opt for a simple difference approach, as explained in the following sections.

The pilot could be implemented at municipal level

Therefore, the pilot implementation could focus on ongoing audits that are similar in terms of type and implementation level to avoid results driven by effects related to these two characteristics. As such, the CGR could select only regular audits implemented at the municipal level as the relevant universe to pilot and assess both measures (A and B).

From this universe, the CGR could select ongoing regular audits across municipalities and assign them into three different groups according to the size and the available resources of the respective municipality to improve comparability between groups. The final composition of the pilot, also depicted in Figure 4.2 could therefore respond to the following logic:

- **Group 1:** A first group of municipal audits is used as the control group. In these audit processes, the measures will not be implemented.

- **Group 2:** In a further group of municipal audits, the meeting (Measure A) will be implemented without the possibility to allow for flexible deadlines (Measure B).

- **Group 3:** Finally, in a third group of municipal audits, both the meeting (Measure A) and flexible deadlines (Measure B) will be implemented.

Figure 4.2. Implementation design of the pilot interventions

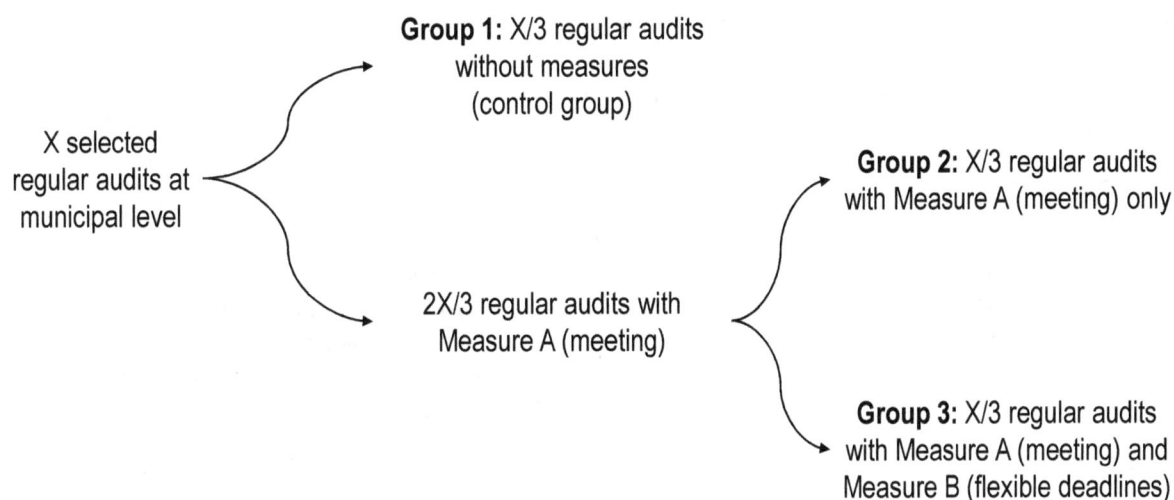

Group 1: X/3 regular audits without measures (control group)

X selected regular audits at municipal level

2X/3 regular audits with Measure A (meeting)

Group 2: X/3 regular audits with Measure A (meeting) only

Group 3: X/3 regular audits with Measure A (meeting) and Measure B (flexible deadlines)

Note: Groups are balanced in terms of size and budgets of municipalities.

Change could be measured through surveys and the implementation rate

To assess the effects of the meetings and flexible deadlines, relevant outcomes of these three groups will be compared through a simple difference approach. This means that the impact of the meeting (Measure A) is measured as the difference between group #2 and #1, and the relative impact of flexible deadlines (Measure B) as the difference between group #3 and #1.

To measure the effects of these two interventions, three surveys could be designed and sent respectively to auditors, public managers (auditees) and Directors of Internal Control. These surveys should ask for perception and attitudes of the three groups to test the underlying mechanisms represented in Figure 4.1 that could drive the behavioural change and positively impact on the uptake of the audit reports. Given sufficient time, the impact of the implemented measures could be measured directly at the level of the rate of implementation.

In fact, the CGR could consider introducing regular surveys amongst stakeholders. These could build on this pilot exercise and the questions that were used. Several SAI use such type of surveys. Box 4.1 provides some examples of client surveys conducted by SAI's to improve their understanding of auditees' perceptions. However, it is important to take due care of not creating a too strong client-relationship with auditees or generating potential "revenge" responses from audited services.

Box 4.1. Supreme Audit Institutions that survey key users to assess quality of audit work

Australia

After each performance audit report is complete, the Australian National Audit Office (ANAO) seeks feedback on the audit process by means of a survey and an interview with the responsible manager of the audited entity. The survey is an important tool for improving the quality and effectiveness of performance audit services. Survey results provide an insight into the effectiveness of current practice and inform the development of new audit practices and approaches. The survey is designed by a firm of consultants that is engaged by the ANAO but independent of the performance audit teams. The response rate from auditees surveyed for the 2011–12 reporting period was 75% and 87% in 2010-11.

Key matters on which feedback is sought include the audit process; audit reporting; and the value of the ANAO's performance audit services more generally. For instance, in the 2011-12 survey, the proportion of respondents that acknowledged the value added by ANAO services was 91% (up from 86% in 2010–11). The percentage of respondents that considered the auditors had demonstrated the professional knowledge and audit skills required to conduct the audit was 85% (down from 91% in 2010-11).

Denmark

Rigsrevisionen, the SAI of Denmark, has used a variety of techniques to assess its benefits to audited entities and to the governance system, including client surveys. For instance, in 2009, Rigsrevisionen hired a consultancy firm to conduct an independent client survey on their behalf. The clients included permanent secretaries, director generals, managing directors of government-owned companies, financial managers, other officials in central government and members of the Parliament's Public Accounts Committee.

Rigsrevisionen officials were most interested in understanding how their clients experienced the quality of services offered, their working relationship and the usefulness of their audit findings. The survey identified areas for improvement across four areas: financial auditing (annual audit); performance auditing (major examinations); co-ordination, planning and counselling; and interaction with the Public Accounts Committee. The findings included recommendations to become more responsive during the audit phase in which memoranda and draft reports are being prepared, and to raise the competencies of SAI staff to a more uniform level.

New Zealand

The New Zealand Office of the Auditor General (OAG) uses an independent firm to conduct an annual client satisfaction survey of public entities audited by the Auditor General. The firm surveys a random sample of public entities to measure the level of satisfaction and identify areas where OAG needs to improve their audit services. Before 2007/08, the survey sample was confined to public entities audited by OAG. In 2007/08, OAG extended the sample to cover public entities audited by private sector accounting firms. Representatives of a sample of these entities are invited to participate in a telephone interview to provide comment and to rate the following factors on a scale from 1 to 10, with 1 being very low and 10 being very high:

- audit service providers' core audit ability
- audit service providers' staff knowledge
- the way audit service providers' staff work with entities, including governing bodies and audit committees where relevant
- the value that audit service providers add and the usefulness of the advice given
- the performance and contribution that audit service providers made as entities prepared to adopt New Zealand Equivalents to International Financial Reporting Standards (NZ IFRS) the overall degree of satisfaction with the service received from audit service provider.

The results of client surveys are prominently displayed in OAG's annual reports, including in the preface by the Auditor General. Doing so communicates the importance of the surveys to OAG staff, as well as alertness among the leadership of the importance of meeting stakeholders' and clients' evolving needs.

Source: OECD (2014[3]), *Chile's Supreme Audit Institution: Enhancing Strategic Agility and Public Trust*, OECD Public Governance Reviews, OECD Publishing, Paris, http://dx.doi.org/10.1787/9789264207561-en; New Zealand Controller and Auditor-General (2009[4]), "Annual Report 2008-2009", Office of the Auditor-General, New Zealand, www.oag.govt.nz/2009/2008-09/docs/annual-report.pdf.

References

Johnsøn, J. (2012), *Theories of change in anti-corruption work: A tool for programme design and evaluation*, Chr. Michelsen Institute (U4 Issue 2012:6), Bergen, http://www.cmi.no/publications/publication/?4635=theories-of-change-in-anti-corruption-work.   [1]

New Zealand Controller and Auditor-General (2009), "Annual Report 2008-2009", Office of the Auditor-General, New Zealand, http://www.oag.govt.nz/2009/2008-09/docs/annual-report.pdf.   [4]

OECD (2017), *Monitoring and Evaluating Integrity Policies*, Working Party of Senior Public Integrity Officials GOV/PGC/INT(2017)4, Paris.   [2]

OECD (2014), *Chile's Supreme Audit Institution: Enhancing Strategic Agility and Public Trust*, OECD Public Governance Reviews, OECD Publishing, Paris, https://doi.org/10.1787/9789264207561-en.   [3]

www.ingramcontent.com/pod-product-compliance
Lightning Source LLC
Chambersburg PA
CBHW081202270326
41930CB00014B/3267